ECO-VACATIONS

Enjoy Yourself and Save the Earth

by
Evelyn Kaye

🐧 BLUE PENGUIN PUBLICATIONS

This book is printed on recycled paper.

Eco-vacations
Enjoy Yourself and Save the Earth
by Evelyn Kaye

Published by
Blue Penguin Publications
147 Sylvan Avenue
Leonia NJ 07605

All rights reserved. No part of this book may be reproduced or transmitted in any form or by any means, electronic or mechanical, including photocopying, recording or by any information storage and retrieval system without written permission from the author, except for the inclusion of brief quotations in a review.

Every effort has been made to ensure the accuracy of the information in this book. But the world of travel is subject to constant change. The publishers take no responsibility for any inaccuracies relating to the material included. Readers are urged to contact the organizations directly before making travel plans.

COPYRIGHT 1991 by Evelyn Kaye
First Printing 1991.
Printed in the United States of America.

ISBN 0-9626231-1-3
Library of Congress Catalog No: 91-070296

Contents

Acknowledgements 5
Introduction 7
    How to Use This Book 11
    Eco-Vacationers Quiz 14
Program Topics 19
    Air Pollution 20
    Animals and Birds 22
    Archaeology and History 25
    Cities 28
    Flowers, Land, Plants, Trees . . . 31
    Human Relations 35
    Lakes, Rivers, Oceans 38
    Scientific Research 41
Programs within the United States 44
Programs outside the United States 47
Parks: Local, State, National 50
Wilderness Areas 53
Children Welcome 57
Organizations A to Z 61
Appendix 225
Index 237

The Author

EVELYN KAYE, traveler, writer, and publisher is always ready to take off and see the world. She has traveled throughout the United States, and in Canada, England, Scotland, France, Italy, Israel, the Netherlands, Sweden, Ecuador, Mexico, Australia, and New Zealand. She's sailed round the Galapagos Islands, hiked hut-to-hut in the White Mountains, river-rafted in the Grand Canyon, and walked across extinct volcanoes in Hawaii.

A published author, her books include *Travel and Learn: The New Guide to Educational Travel; Family Guide to Cape Cod; College Bound; Crosscurrents: The Hole in the Sheet;* and *How to Treat TV with TLC.* Her articles have appeared in *Travel & Leisure, Adventure Travel, McCalls, Parents, New York*, and *Glamour*, as well as the *New York Times, Boston Globe,* and *NJ Record.* She was a reporter for the *(Manchester) Guardian* and for Reuters News Agency in Paris.

She has served as President of the American Society of Journalists and Authors, the leading organization of nonfiction writers in the United States, and as Director of the ASJA Annual Writers' Conference in New York City. She is a member of several environmental organizations and is an active hiker.

Introduction 5

Acknowledgements

No author works entirely alone, and many people provided assistance as I wrote this book.

Sincere thanks to the environmental organizations for providing materials, answering questions and completing questionnaires. Karen Christenson sent me clippings from her writing on the Green movement, and environmentalists gave me suggestions and ideas.

My appreciation to members of the American Society of Journalists and Authors for their encouragement, in particular to Grace Weinstein, Roberta Roesch, Lois Libien, Toni Goldfarb, Anne Finger, Penny Colman, and good memories of June Roth. Also, my thanks to the self-publishing community whose advice I took, in particular Dan Poynter, Marilyn Ross, John Kremer, and Barbara Brabec.

Thanks to Janet Gardner, who read the first part of the book and gave me valuable advice. Many thanks to Claudia Caruana who copyedited the text. Katrina Sarson and Nick Morris in Chicago sent suggestions for promotion. David Sarson and Lisa Harrington provided

6 Eco-Vacations

research in Colorado. And a hug to Claire Josephine Harrington Sarson, making a first appearance in print.

Finally, my deepest appreciation to my Blue Penguin partner and friend Christopher Sarson, who not only provides sound critical advice about the book, but understands how to talk to computers so they don't flash in your face. He guided us successfully through all the technical stages of this project, from Error messages to the final printed pages. Here's to the next book!

Eco-Vacations was written on an IBM-compatible computer, using Wordperfect 5.1, Digifonts typefaces, and a HP LaserJet III printer. The book was printed by Bookcrafters on acid-free recycled paper.

Introduction 7

Introduction

"Climb the mountains and get their good tidings. Nature's peace will flow into you as sunshine flows into trees." John Muir

This book offers a new approach to vacations. It's designed to show you how to plan a vacation from an environmental point of view.

As I travel around, I've become more and more aware of how environmental damage affects not only the way we live, but also the way we take our vacations. I've seen seashores polluted by oil slicks in California, Alaska, Europe, Africa, and Asia. I know poisonous smog blankets cities like Mexico City and Los Angeles, Bucharest and Tokyo. In the pristine beauty of the Rocky Mountains I've been warned that the water in the rushing streams is no longer safe to drink.

There are people who feel that worrying about environmental issues has nothing to do with vacations. A vacation is the one time to escape, take a break, forget the pressures of daily life. You hear enough about the troubles of the world the rest of the time.

8 Eco-Vacations

Well, as the song says, the times they are a-changing. Millions of us go on vacation and what we choose to do affects the air and water and land and the places we visit as much as what we do the rest of the year. If we take a bus or train across country instead of driving a car, we show a new environmental awareness. If we visit a national park and take care to leave it as clean and peaceful as we found it, we are acting in an environmentally positive way.

An Eco-Vacation takes into consideration the impact our travels will have on the air, earth, and sea. The significance of an Eco-Vacation is that it benefits the environment as well as providing a break from routine.

There are two styles of Eco-Vacation. First, you can choose activities which don't pollute. You can go hiking, biking, camping, walking, paddling a canoe, windsurfing, or sailing. Try kayaking in Baja and see the remaining humpback whales which migrate there every winter. Explore Alaska on foot to be dazzled by summer wildflowers on the tundra, and better understand the dangers of oil drilling in the region.

Second, you can take an active part in preserving what we have. You can join scientists studying dolphin behavior to learn what is needed to assure their survival in the ocean. You can help maintain hiking trails by clearing trees, building bridges, and taking out trash. You can assist rangers in state and national parks by

Introduction 9

leading nature walks to teach people respect for the wilderness. You can rebuild ancient buildings in villages in Europe to preserve them for the future.

An Eco-Vacation gives you a chance to do something positive for the earth. It will make you feel good, and counter the pressures of everyday life. What you decide to do will make a difference. An Eco-Vacation is an experience designed to enrich and expand your understanding of the world. And, according to those who've tried it, you'll have a great time.

An Eco-Vacation can be as relaxed or as rugged as you want. It will show you new places and new experiences. On one program, you spend a month in South India sharing the daily life of a village in harmony with the environment. On another, you canoe the peaceful waters of Georgia's Okefenokee Swamp to see basking alligators, graceful wading birds, and cypress forests.

Information about Eco-Vacations is difficult to find. That's why I decided to write this book. Here in one volume is everything you need to know about hundreds of Eco-Vacations around the world. You'll be able to pick the perfect way to go biking in Europe, work on trail-clearing in Colorado, save turtles in the Virgin Islands, among scores of others programs.

The organizations included in this book were carefully selected. I sent questionnaires to hundreds of groups,

10 Eco-Vacations

and those that replied and were included in the book met the following criteria. Every organization:

· is based in the United States.
· has a strong commitment to environmental ethics.
· has a history of concern for the environment.
· offers programs that abide by environmental rules.
· has leaders who are qualified naturalists, environmentalists, scientists, or professionals in their field.
· has been in operation for several years.
· welcomes inquiries and questions.
· sends full details of programs plus other information.
· has letters and evaluations from former participants.
· has an active office and answers the phone.

The book provides full details of every organization with name, address, phone and fax number, descriptions of programs, price range, and qualifications needed. All you have to do is decide where and when you'd like to go. To help you with the decision, take the Eco-Vacation Quiz to find out what suits you best.

Please drop me a line to let me know about your experiences. I'd love to hear what you found on this brand-new style of vacation. And do send me your suggestions for places and programs to include in future editions of the book. Happy Eco-travels!

Evelyn Kaye

Introduction 11

How To Use This Book

The book is organized into two sections:

Program Topics.
Here are descriptions of the different topics related to Eco-Vacations, so you can choose those that interest you, together with a list of the organizations offering them.

Organizations.
This section provides an alphabetical list of every organization offering Eco-Vacations. Here are details of programs, address, phone, fax, contact name, price range, and what's included.

At the end of each Organization's listing, there's additional information.

Age range.
Most trips are designed for people of all ages, but some do attract a majority of older people or

12 Eco-Vacations

younger people. This information is based on people who've taken trips before.

Children.
Many programs welcome children. Some organizations have facilities for infants and toddlers, some accept youngsters over 8, and some only accept children over 16.

Qualifications.
You may have to join the organization and pay a membership fee. A few programs request special skills. Some outdoor programs require experience in backpacking, hiking, or active outdoor activity, and require a health certificate to show you are in good physical condition.

Price range.
The two figures listed in this section are the lowest and highest prices for the programs offered. Prices vary widely depending on services provided and how long the program runs. Also, while every effort has been made to give you the most accurate information available, prices can change. Check with the organizations.

Price includes.
Here again, programs vary. The travel costs may include airfare, or you may have to pay airfare to the starting point. The price may include accommo-

dations, all meals, guides and lectures, or you may be expected to bring along food and camping equipment. Ask what the costs cover so you know what's included.

Participants provide.
Most often you only have to bring along personal items. But it's good to know if you have to provide some meals or camping equipment yourself.

Once you've selected your program topics, contact the organizations for brochures. Call if you have questions, and then book your trip.

14 Eco-Vacations

Eco-Vacationer's Quiz

Take this personal quiz to help you evaluate your skills, your interests, and your abilities. Find out if your passion for research in the jungle coincides with the realization that there will be large spiders in your tent!

Age is unimportant; there are 90 year olds exploring the Polar icecap, 60 year olds digging up archaeological remains, and 40 year olds taking up sailing. Men and women join environmental programs with equal success.

Assess your abilities, add a large dollop of enthusiasm, and you'll be able to do virtually anything you want, regardless of your background, education, age, sex, or anxiety quotient.

Introduction 15

HEALTH

Be honest about your physical abilities. Sitting at a desk all day and getting out of breath climbing the stairs indicates you need to start an exercise program before you even think about climbing Mount Rainier. At the same time, don't sell yourself short if you exercise regularly even if you can't run the marathon.

· What kind of physical condition am I in? . . . .
. . . .

· How much do I exercise on a regular basis? . .
. . . .

· Can I carry a backpack? . . . .

· Any medical problems? . . . .

· Am I affected by:
high altitudes . . . .
heat or humidity . . . .
desert dryness . . . .
damp and cold . . . .
noise . . . .
bad smells . . . .
dirt . . . .

16 Eco-Vacations

EXPERIENCE

Your activities and interests reflect the kind of environmental vacation that you will enjoy. Your fascination with computers may help scientists on a project analyzing the composition of fossils. Your skills at interviewing are ideal for research into the effects of air pollution on a community. Your certification as a lifesaver is welcome aboard a boat observing whales and dolphins.

Check your experience with activities you've tried. :

Biking	Lifesaving . . . .
Birding	Mountain climbing . . .
Boating	Painting . . . .
Camping	Photography . . . .
Canoeing	Publishing . . . .
Computers	Rowing . . . .
Drawing	Scuba . . . .
Drive jeep/van	Snorkeling . . . .
Filmmaking	Swimming . . . .
Gardening	Tree care . . . .
Hiking	Video . . . .
Interviewing	Wildlife studies . . . . .
Kayaking	Writing . . . .

Any special skills? . . . .

PERSONAL

Think about how you would cope with an environmental vacation. Are you ready to camp out miles from civilization or would you prefer a cabin near a campground? Will you panic when plans change? How do you feel about eating strange foods?

What do I want from an Eco-Vacation? . . . .
. . . .
. . . .

Now ask how you would rate yourself on a scale of 5=Terrific 4=Good 3=OK 2=Fair 1=Count me out, for:
Sense of adventure . . . .
Sense of humor . . . .
Optimism . . . .
Energy . . . .
Ability to adapt to unknown circumstances . . . .
Tolerance for sharing sleeping accommodation .
Ability to get on with different people . . . .
Ability to cope with a crisis . . . .
Flexibility when plans change suddenly . . . . . .
Presenting a positive attitude at all times . . . . .
Ability to keep calm in danger . . . .
Ability to laugh at yourself . . . .

TOTAL number of points . . . .

18 Eco-Vacations

WHAT YOUR PERSONAL SCORE MEANS

Under 25. Communal life in the wilderness may not be for you. You'll be happier with your own tent, or on educational programs in lodges, inns, or hotels.

26 to 40. You're honest, adaptable and easy-going, and will feel comfortable on most group environmental programs.

Over 40. You are ideally suited for challenging outdoor ecology programs and will enjoy all of them.

On this quiz, there are no winners and no perfect scores. Look back at your answers. They should be a guide to discovering the kind of environmental vacation you would find most enjoyable.

Programs 19

Program Topics

In the pages ahead you'll find descriptions of the many varieties of eco-vacations available. This section is designed to help you find a vacation that meshes with your interests.

Program topics include: Air Pollution; Animals and Birds; Archaeology and History; Cities; Flowers, Land, Plants, Trees; Human Relations; Lakes, Rivers, Oceans; and Scientific Research. There are four geographical categories: programs in the United States, outside the United States, in parks, and in wilderness areas. Also, programs where children are welcome.

Take your time as you browse through the descriptions. At the end of each one is a list of the organizations which offer vacation programs related to the topics.

If you have questions, don't hesitate to call the organizations listed with the topic. Good organizations want to make sure you have the best experience possible and provide detailed background materials about their programs on request.

20 Eco-Vacations

Air Pollution

No matter where you travel, the effects of polluted air can be a hazard. In the Grand Canyon, winds sometimes sweep polluted air across the canyon so that the magnificent views are clouded by haze and dust. You can join programs to study its effects.

In Sweden, there's a special two-week seminar on the environment in relation to conservation, waste collection, recycling, the greenhouse effect, and air pollution. In Switzerland, you spend time in an Ecology Center in the Alps and work on environmental programs related to the region.

To help reduce air pollution, take a bike trip. One European biking tour travels through the Netherlands, Belgium and reunited Germany. Another explores Africa to emphasize the importance of bicycle-friendly transportation. And others travel through California and Connecticut, Michigan and Massachusetts, New Jersey and New Mexico. For hikers, walkers, and trekkers, there are dozens of outdoor experiences offered by different groups to see some of the most spectacular scenery in the world.

List of Organizations

American Youth Hostels
Appalachian Mountain Club
Arizona State Parks
Backroads Bicycle Touring
Canoe Country Escapes
Earthwatch Expeditions
Eco-Tourism International
Gerhard's Bicycle Odysseys
International Bicycle Fund
International Bicycle Tours
Marine Sciences Under Sails
National Society for Internships
National Wildlife Federation
Offshore Sailing School
People to People International
Population-Environment Balance
Student Conservation Association
Volunteers for Peace
Washington State Senior Environmental Corps
World Wildlife Fund

22 Eco-Vacations

Animals and Birds

There are wildlife programs around the world where unique species still live in their natural surroundings. You can visit many of these places on naturalist tours.

On research programs, you can help with dozens of fascinating projects. In South Carolina, you can study the diamondback terrapins to examine how these animals meet, mate, and grow. You can look for dolphins in Florida's Tampa and Sarasota Bays to document and videotape their behavior and establish a database of information. Off the coast of Cape Cod, you can study the egg-laying habits of the horseshoe crab with its strange helmet-shaped carapace.

In Queensland, Australia, researchers examine how koala bears live in the forest and eat eucalyptus leaves from dusk to dawn. In Indonesia, researchers record the behavior of Bali Temple Monkeys as they search for food. In Mexico researchers examine the effects of the hurricane of 1988 on the parrots, toucans, spoonbills, herons, pelicans, and migratory flocks in the region.

Programs 23

List of Organizations

Alaska Discovery
American Cetacean Society
American Hiking Society
American Museum of Natural History
American Wilderness Experience
Arctic Odysseys
Arctic Treks
Arizona Raft Adventures
Backroads Bicycle Touring
Baja Expeditions
California State Polytechnic University
Camp Denali/North Face Lodge
Canoe Country Escapes
Canyonlands Field Institute
Cornell's Adult University
Earthwatch Expeditions
Eco-Tourism International
Eye of the Whale
Florida Oceanographic Society
Florida State Parks
Foundation for Field Research
International Expeditions
International Research Expeditions
International Zoological Expeditions
Journeys
Marine Sciences Under Sails
Massachusetts Audubon Society
Mountain Travel

24 Eco-Vacations

National Audubon Society
National Society for Internships
National Wildlife Federation
Natural Habitat
Nature Expeditions International
New York Botanical Garden
North Cascades Institute
Oceanic Society Expeditions
Overseas Adventure Travel
Pacific Northwest Field Seminars
Questers
Rainbow Adventures
San Jose State University
Sierra Club
Smithsonian Research Expeditions
Sobek Expeditions
Society Expeditions
Southern Cross Expeditions/Brazil
Student Conservation Association
Trans-Pacific Special Interest Tours
University Research Expeditions Program
USDA Forest Service
Washington State Senior Environmental Corps
Wild Horizons Expeditions
Wilderness Southeast
Wildlands Studies/SFSU
Womantrek
World Wildlife Fund
Yellowstone Institute
Zoetic Research

Archaeology and History

Preserving history is as much a part of ecological action as caring for the natural world. There are projects in many parts of the world, some close to cities, some in wilderness areas, where volunteer assistance is welcomed.

Only a few miles from New York City there's a study of the oldest shell refuse mound on the Atlantic Coast, dating back nearly 7,000 years. It's at Dogan Point in the Lower Hudson River Valley, near Croton-on-Hudson. Shells, bones, hearths, tools, plant and other cultural remains have been found. The project's thesis is that changes in cultural behavior began at the coast, and moved north and inland, reversing the currently accepted theory. You join researchers and excavate, water screen, take photographs, make drawings, map, probe, and sample soil.

In the west, archaeologists excavate sites related to the lives of the Anasazi Indians in the Four Corners region of Colorado to discover why the Anasazi left at the end of the 13th century and never returned. You join them on this long-term project to dig and explore the region.

26 Eco-Vacations

Alamos in Mexico was once the center of a rich mining region. Many of its old buildings are still standing. Today researchers are documenting the many examples of 18th and 19th century Spanish Colonial architecture with interior galleries, decorative window grilles, and hand-carved panelled doors.

You can tour ancient cities on a walking tour of northern England and Wales, where footpaths lead to settlements dating back to Roman times. And in France and Italy, volunteers learn traditional building techniques and work on restoring and reconstructing the houses and churches of medieval villages.

List of Organizations

American Hiking Society
American Museum of Natural History
American Wilderness Experience
Arctic Odysseys
Arizona State Parks
Canoe Country Escapes
Canyonlands Field Institute
Crow Canyon Archaeological Center
Earthwatch Expeditions
Eco-Tourism International
Florida Oceanographic Society
Florida State Parks
Foundation for Field Research
Gerhard's Bicycle Odysseys

Programs 27

Global Exchange Reality Tours
International Bicycle Fund
International Bicycle Tours
International Expeditions
International Research Expeditions
Journeys
La Sabranenque
Marine Sciences Under Sails
National Audubon Society
National Society for Internships
Nature Expeditions International
North Cascades Institute
Overseas Adventure Travel
Pacific Northwest Field Seminars
Rainbow Adventures
San Jose State University
Sierra Club
Smithsonian Research Expeditions
Sobek Expeditions
Society Expeditions
Student Conservation Association
Trans-Pacific Special Interest Tours
University Research Expeditions Program
USDA Forest Service
Volunteers for Peace
Womantrek
Yellowstone Institute

28 Eco-Vacations

Cities

Not all environmental vacations focus on the wilderness or regions far from civilization. Some programs examine the environment and pollution in cities and suburban areas.

You can attend a program in Budapest and Prague to study the transformation of the economic landscape and its effect on the ecology, politics, social policy, and foreign policy in Hungary and Czechoslovakia.

Programs comparing the environmental efforts in Sweden and the United States are offered in Stockholm. Workcamp programs in Europe and Asia are based in towns to work on environmental issues.

Other city-based programs support nature centers and gardening projects to help preserve open land in developed areas. Some set up observation surveys to monitor air and water content. And on tours of historic cities, there are often special seminars on the effects of pollution on statues and buildings.

Programs 29

List of Organizations

American Museum of Natural History
American Youth Hostels
Appalachian Mountain Club
Backroads Bicycle Touring
Center for Responsible Tourism
Clearwater Inc.
Cornell's Adult University
Earthwatch Expeditions
Florida Oceanographic Society
Florida State Parks
Food First Institute
Gerhard's Bicycle Odysseys
Global Exchange Reality Tours
Habitat for Humanity International
International Bicycle Fund
International Bicycle Tours
International Research Expeditions
Journeys
Lisle Fellowship
Marine Sciences Under Sails
Mobility International USA
Mountain Travel
National Audubon Society
National Society for Internships
Oceanic Society Expeditions
People to People International
Population-Environment Balance
Questers

30 Eco-Vacations

San Jose State University
Smithsonian Research Expeditions
Southern Cross Expeditions/Brazil
Student Conservation Association
Trans-Pacific Special Interest Tours
University Research Expeditions Program
Volunteers for Peace
Washington State Senior Environmental Corps
Womantrek
World Wildlife Fund

Programs 31

Flowers, Plants, Land, Trees

The natural world offers the widest diversity for environmental trips. You can visit the Great Barrier Reef in Australia and marvel at the beauty of its underwater coral reef, study wildflowers in the Rocky Mountains, visit the gardens of England, or see the unique trees and plants of the Galapagos Islands.

Researchers can help in Hawaii's Volcanoes National Park to collect data on bird and plant life; once only large trees survived the rooting pigs and browsing goats until the National Park Service eliminated them and regeneration began.

Florida and many other states welcome volunteers in state parks. Florida's 14 parks have acres of salt marsh, pine flatwoods, and sand pine scrub.

You can join a program in the tropical rainforest to study the diversity of plants and trees in the region. You can study the return of the plants and flowers to Yellowstone National Park after the fire. And you can join the Children's Farm in Belgium to introduce city children to work on the land where they grow vegetables and flowers.

32 Eco-Vacations

List of Organizations

Alaska Discovery
American Hiking Society
American Horticultural Society
American Museum of Natural History
American Wilderness Experience
American Youth Hostels
Appalachian Mountain Club
Arctic Odysseys
Arctic Treks
Arizona Raft Adventures
Arizona State Parks
Backroads Bicycle Touring
Baja Expeditions
California State Polytechnic University
Camp Denali/North Face Lodge
Canoe Country Escapes
Canyonlands Field Institute
Center for Responsible Tourism
Clearwater Inc.
Colorado Trail Foundation
Cornell's Adult University
Crow Canyon Archaeological Center
Earthwatch Expeditions
Eco-Tourism International
Eye of the Whale
Florida Oceanographic Society
Florida State Parks
Food First Institute

Programs 33

Foundation for Field Research
Gerhard's Bicycle Odysseys
Global Exchange Reality Tours
Foundation for Field Research
International Bicycle Fund
International Bicycle Tours
International Expeditions
International Research Expeditions
International Zoological Expeditions
Journeys
La Sabranenque
Lost Coast Llama Caravans
Marine Sciences Under Sails
Mobility International
National Audubon Society
National Society for Internships
National Wildlife Federation
Nature Expeditions International
New York Botanical Garden
North Cascades Institute
Oceanic Society Adventures
Overseas Adventure Travel
Pacific Northwest Field Seminars
People to People International
Questers
Rainbow Adventures
San Jose State University
Sierra Club
Smithsonian Research Expeditions
Sobek Expeditions

Society Expeditions
Student Conservation Association
Trans-Pacific Special Interest Tours
University Research Expeditions Program
USDA Forest Service
Volunteers for Peace
Washington State Senior Environmental Corps
Wild Horizons Expeditions
Wilderness Preservation
Wildlands Studies/SFSU
Womantrek
World Wildlife Fund
Yellowstone Institute
Zoetic Research

Programs 35

Human Relations

You can choose to work with people to help them understand the impact of ecology. When you travel off the beaten track to learn about different communities, you expand your knowledge of the way other people balance their styles of living and ecological concerns.

In southern India, you can spend a month immersed in the daily routines of a village where the lifestyle is in harmony with the environment. It's a democratic community with a high literacy rate and strong political involvement. You stay with a family, eat meals with them, share their lives, and attend seminars.

International workcamps offer an opportunity to work together with people from many different backgrounds. In the town of Marzabotto in Italy, where the Nazis massacred 900 people, you can join a workcamp for peace and international cooperation. You can live in a Benedictine monastery in the Netherlands taking part in the daily life of contemplation and working on chores for four hours a day.

36 Eco-Vacations

List of Organizations

American Hiking Society
American Youth Hostels
Arctic Odysseys
Arizona Raft Adventures
Arizona State Parks
Earthwatch Expeditions
Food First Institute
Foundation for Field Research
Global Exchange Reality Tours
Habitat for Humanity International
International Bicycle Fund
International Bicycle Tours
International Expeditions
International Research Expeditions
Journeys
Lisle Fellowship
Marine Sciences Under Sails
Mobility International USA
National Audubon Society
National Society for Internships
National Wildlife Federation
Offshore Sailing School
Overseas Adventure Travel
People to People International
Population-Environment Balance
Questers
San Jose State University
Smithsonian Research Expeditions

Society Expeditions
Trans-Pacific Special Interest Tours
University Research Expeditions Program
Volunteers for Peace
Wildlands Studies/SFSU
World Wildlife Fund
Yellowstone Institute

38 Eco-Vacations

Lakes, Rivers, Oceans

A sailing ship explores the shoreline of Turkey as part of a non-polluting tour of a historic region while overnight moorings savor the food and hospitality of modern Turkish life in fishing villages and harbors along the way.

River-rafting trips add the excitement of whitewater rapids. Float through the drama of the Colorado River in the Grand Canyon, or along the rivers of California, Utah, and Arizona.

You can swim with dolphins in the Bahamas and use video and acoustic recording equipment to collect information on their communication systems and habitat. Aboard a ship in Southeast Alaska you can study humpback whales in their feeding grounds near the glaciers. Sailing around the Galapagos Islands, you'll visit rocky shores to see blue-footed boobies, marine iguanas, red-billed tropic birds, and sea lions.

Programs 39

List of Organizations

American Cetacean Society
American Hiking Society
American Museum of Natural History
American Wilderness Experience
Arctic Odysseys
Arctic Treks
Arizona Raft Adventures
Arizona State Parks
Baja Expeditions
California State Polytechnic University
Camp Denali/North Face Lodge
Canoe Country Escapes
Canyonlands Field Institute
Center for Responsible Tourism
Clearwater Inc.
Earthwatch Expeditions
Eco-Tourism International
Eye of the Whale
Florida Oceanographic Society
Florida State Parks
Global Exchange Reality Tours
Foundation for Field Research
International Expeditions
International Research Expeditions
International Zoological Expeditions
Journeys
Marine Sciences Under Sails
National Society for Internships

40 Eco-Vacations

National Wildlife Federation
New York Botanical Garden
Oceanic Society Expeditions
Offshore Sailing School
Overseas Adventure Travel
Pacific Northwest Field Seminars
People to People International
Population-Environment Balance
Questers
Rainbow Adventures
San Jose State University
Sierra Club
Sobek Expeditions
Society Expeditions
Student Conservation Association
Trans-Pacific Special Interest Tours
University Research Expeditions Program
USDA Forest Service
Volunteers for Peace
Washington State Senior Environmental Corps
Wild Horizons Expeditions
Wilderness Southeast
Wildlands Studies/SFSU
Womantrek
World Wildlife Fund
Yellowstone Institute
Zoar Outdoor
Zoetic Research

Scientific Research

"The young research assistant Andre and I set off in the darkness at 4 a.m. to check the traps - 200 small metal box traps, each invitingly baited the day before with oats. I also carry the clipboard with the data sheet and plastic bag of tools; tiny numbered ear tags, a small scale to weigh little animals, plastic vials to collect feces from nervous animals, a clipper for the dainty toes of shrews, and a thick plastic bag to hold animals if we should find any. We do; 16 mice, 2 shrews, and a lovely flying squirrel. We take a long time with the squirrel, admiring its elegance and strength."

This account by a volunteer in the Shenandoah Valley, Virginia, describes the research needed to discover whether the food available in fall and winter was enough for the wildlife population of deer, mice, chipmunks, squirrels, and turkeys. You too join a similar expedition, and contribute to the sum of human knowledge. You pay your expenses, which vary depending on the expedition.

Some programs need special qualifications. For assisting with the excavation of a site where the Romans lived in

42 Eco-Vacations

146 BC, you need a knowledge of late Roman history, drawing, photography, and art history. For a research project working with the Ainu, an island tribe in Japan, you need interests in gardening, botany, cultural change, and aboriginal rights. Other programs welcome anyone with energy and enthusiasm.

List of Organizations

American Hiking Society
Arctic Odysseys
California State Polytechnic University
Camp Denali/North Face Lodge
Canyonlands Field Institute
Clearwater Inc.
Crow Canyon Archaeological Center
Earthwatch Expeditions
Eco-Tourism International
Eye of the Whale
Florida Oceanographic Society
Florida State Parks
Foundation for Field Research
International Research Expeditions
International Zoological Expeditions
Journeys
Massachusetts Audubon Society
National Audubon Society
National Society for Internships
National Wildlife Federation
New York Botanical Garden

Oceanic Society Expeditions
Smithsonian Research Expeditions
Southern Cross Expeditions/Brazil
Student Conservation Association
University Research Expeditions Program
USDA Forest Service
Volunteers for Peace
Washington State Senior Environmental Corps
Wildlands Studies/SFSU
World Wildlife Fund
Zoetic Research

44 Eco-Vacations

Programs Within the United States

Hundreds of programs are offered in the United States, in almost every state and in every kind of location. You can join hiking, biking and camping programs in New England, the Midwest, the Far West, or on the Pacific Ocean. You can clear trails in Colorado and Connecticut. You can work on scientific research in Hawaii, Missouri, or Montana. You can explore the bayous of Louisiana, the Pine Barrens of New Jersey, the mountains of Oregon, the deserts of Nevada.

List of Organizations

Alaska Discovery
American Cetacean Society
American Hiking Society
American Horticultural Society
American Museum of Natural History
American Wilderness Experience
American Youth Hostels
Appalachian Mountain Club
Arctic Odysseys
Arctic Treks
Arizona Raft Adventures
Arizona State Parks

Programs 45

Backroads Bicycle Touring
Camp Denali/North Face Lodge
Canoe Country Escapes
Canyonlands Field Institute
Center for Responsible Tourism
Clearwater Inc.
Colorado Trail Foundation
Cornell's Adult University
Crow Canyon Archaeological Center
Earthwatch Expeditions
Eco-Tourism International
Eye of the Whale
Florida Oceanographic Society
Florida State Parks
Food First Institute
Foundation for Field Research
Global Exchange Reality Tours
Habitat for Humanity International
International Bicycle Fund
International Bicycle Tours
International Expeditions
International Research Expeditions
Journeys
Lisle Fellowship
Lost Coast Llama Caravans
Marine Sciences Under Sails
Massachusetts Audubon Society
Mobility International USA
Mountain Travel
National Audubon Society

46 Eco-Vacations

National Society for Internships
National Wildlife Federation
Natural Habitat
Nature Expeditions International
North Cascades Institute
Oceanic Society Expeditions
Offshore Sailing School
Pacific Northwest Field Seminars
Population-Environment Balance
Questers
Rainbow Adventures
Sierra Club Outings
Smithsonian Research Expeditions
Sobek Expeditions
Society Expeditions
Student Conservation Association
Trans-Pacific Special Interest Tours
University Research Expeditions Program
USDA Forest Service
Volunteers for Peace
Washington State Senior Environmental Corps
Wild Horizons Expeditions
Wilderness Southeast
Wildlands Studies/SFSU
Womantrek
World Wildlife Fund
Yellowstone Institute
Zoar Outdoor
Zoetic Research

Programs 47

Programs Outside the United States

Today you can find trips to every corner of the world, for there are almost no places inaccessible to adventurous human beings.

You can tour the glaciers of the Antarctic, swelter in tropical rain forests, or bask on sunbaked beaches. You can visit villages in Europe, Quechua communities in South America, tribes in Africa. You can see the fjords of Norway, the steppes of Russia, the rivers of China, and the Lake District in England.

List of Organizations

Alaska Discovery
American Cetacean Society
American Horticultural Society
American Museum of Natural History
American Wilderness Experience
American Youth Hostels
Arctic Odysseys
Arizona Raft Adventures
Backroads Bicycle Touring
Baja Expeditions
California State Polytechnic University
Center for Responsible Tourism
Cornell's Adult University

48 Eco-Vacations

Earthwatch Expeditions
Eco-Tourism International
Food First Institute
Foundation for Field Research
Gerhard's Bicycle Odysseys
Global Exchange Reality Tours
Habitat for Humanity International
International Bicycle Fund
International Bicycle Tours
International Expeditions
International Research Expeditions
International Zoological Expeditions
Journeys
La Sabranenque
Lisle Fellowship
Marine Sciences Under Sails
Massachusetts Audubon Society
Mobility International USA
Mountain Travel
National Audubon Society
Natural Habitat
Nature Expeditions International
New York Botanical Garden
Oceanic Society Expeditions
Offshore Sailing School
Overseas Adventure Travel
People to People International
Questers
Rainbow Adventures
San Jose State University

Sierra Club Outings
Smithsonian Research Expeditions
Sobek Expeditions
Society Expeditions
Southern Cross Expeditions/Brazil
Trans-Pacific Special Interest Tours
University Research Expeditions Program
Volunteers for Peace
Wilderness Southeast
Wildlands Studies/SFSU
Womantrek
World Wildlife Fund
Zoetic Research

50 Eco-Vacations

Parks: Local, State, and National

One of the only ways to preserve natural areas from development is by creating parklands. Local, state, and national parks reflect the indigenous character of the region, and offer travelers a chance to see trees, flowers, and wildlife in an authentic setting.

You can travel and explore different parklands. In India, you'll find elephants and tigers. In Alaska, there are moose and elk. In California, dramatic mountains and rushing rivers. In Australia, caves with drawings from aboriginal history.

You can join volunteers to help preserve these areas. And you can study aspects of individual parks on scientific research projects. Every park reflects the unique features of the landscape to preserve them for posterity.

List of Organizations

Alaska Discovery
American Hiking Society
American Museum of Natural History

Programs 51

American Wilderness Experience
American Youth Hostels
Appalachian Mountain Club
Arctic Odysseys
Arctic Treks
Arizona Raft Adventures
Arizona State Parks
Backroads Bicycle Touring
Earthwatch Expeditions
Camp Denali/North Face Lodge
Canyonlands Field Institute
Clearwater Inc.
Colorado Trail Foundation
Cornell's Adult University
Eco-Tourism International
Eye of the Whale
Florida Oceanographic Society
Florida State Parks
International Expeditions
International Research Expeditions
International Zoological Expeditions
Journeys
Lost Coast Llama Caravans
Marine Sciences Under Sails
Mobility International USA
Mountain Travel
National Audubon Society
National Society for Internships
National Wildlife Federation
Natural Habitat

52 Eco-Vacations

Nature Expeditions International
North Cascades Institute
Oceanic Society Expeditions
Overseas Adventure Travel
Pacific Northwest Field Seminars
People to People International
Questers
Rainbow Adventures
San Jose State University
Sierra Club Outings
Smithsonian Research Expeditions
Sobek Expeditions
Southern Cross Expeditions/Brazil
Student Conservation Association
Trans-Pacific Special Interest Tours
University Research Expeditions Program
USDA Forest Service
Volunteers for Peace
Washington State Senior Environmental Corps
Wild Horizons Expeditions
Wilderness Southeast
Wildlands Studies/SFSU
Womantrek
World Wildlife Fund
Yellowstone Institute
Zoetic Research

Wilderness Areas

The last wilderness areas in the world, places where human beings have not established the trappings of civilization, are becoming more and more difficult to find. Exploring the wilderness demands a readiness to give up the comforts of everyday life to explore regions that are untouched.

You can spend a week in a lodge in Alaska with no human beings for miles around. You can camp on a deserted beach in Hawaii with the sound of the thundering surf for a lullaby. You can canoe through the Minnesota Boundary waters and hear only the sound of birds above. You can hike through the vastness of the Grand Canyon awed by the splendor of the soaring cliffs.

Despite the difficulties, the urge to escape is strong, and treks to wilderness areas become more popular every year.

54 Eco-Vacations

List of Organizations

Alaska Discovery
American Cetacean Society
American Hiking Society
American Museum of Natural History
American Wilderness Experience
American Youth Hostels
Appalachian Mountain Club
Arctic Odysseys
Arctic Treks
Arizona State Parks
Backroads Bicycle Touring
Baja Expeditions
California State Polytechnic University
Camp Denali/North Face Lodge
Canoe Country Escapes
Canyonlands Field Institute
Center for Responsible Tourism
Colorado Trail Foundation
Cornell's Adult University
Crow Canyon Archaeological Center
Earthwatch Expeditions
Eco-Tourism International
Eye of the Whale
Florida Oceanographic Society
Florida State Parks
Foundation for Field Research
Habitat for Humanity International
International Expeditions

Programs 55

International Research Expeditions
International Zoological Expeditions
Journeys
Lisle Fellowship
Lost Coast Llama Caravans
Massachusetts Audubon Society
Mountain Travel
National Audubon Society
National Society for Internships
National Wildlife Federation
Natural Habitat
Nature Expeditions International
New York Botanical Garden
North Cascades Institute
Oceanic Society Expeditions
Overseas Adventure Travel
Pacific Northwest Field Seminars
People to People International
Questers
Rainbow Adventures
San Jose State University
Sierra Club Outings
Smithsonian Research Expeditions
Sobek Expeditions
Society Expeditions
Southern Cross Expeditions/Brazil
Student Conservation Association
Trans-Pacific Special Interest Tours
University Research Expeditions Program
USDA Forest Service

56 Eco-Vacations

Volunteers for Peace
Washington State Senior Environmental Corps
Wild Horizons Expeditions
Wilderness Southeast
Wildlands Studies/SFSU
Womantrek
World Wildlife Fund
Yellowstone Institute
Zoar Travel
Zoetic Research

Children Welcome

Introducing children to the environment is one of the more rewarding aspects of parenthood. Most children respond honestly to the experience of camping out, watching chipmunks scampering in the woods, exploring a tropical rainforest, or eating dinner by a campfire on a deserted beach.

For families eager to take their children on some of the trips offered in the book, the majority of organizations welcome children accompanied by parents.

A few accept infants and toddlers. Some request that children are over 8 years old, and some that they are over 16. Check if the programs requires certain skills, and make sure the children are old enough to keep up with activities such as hiking or trekking.

List of Organizations

Alaska Discovery
American Cetacean Society
American Hiking Society
American Horticultural Society

58 Eco-Vacations

American Museum of Natural History
American Youth Hostels
Appalachian Mountain Club
Arctic Treks
Arizona Raft Adventures
Backroads Bicycle Touring
Camp Denali/North Face Lodge
Canoe Country Escapes
Canyonlands Field Institute
Center for Responsible Tourism
Clearwater Inc.
Colorado Trail Foundation
Cornell's Adult University
Crow Canyon Archaeological Center
Earthwatch
Eco-Tourism International
Eye of the Whale
Florida Oceanographic Society
Foundation for Field Research
Gerhard's Bicycle Odysseys
International Bicycle Tours
International Zoological Expeditions
Journeys
Marine Sciences Under Sail
Massachusetts Audubon Society
Mobility International USA
Mountain Travel
National Audubon Society
National Wildlife Federation
Natural Habitat

Programs 59

Nature Expeditions International
North Cascades Institute
Oceanic Society Expeditions
Offshore Sailing School
Overseas Adventure Travel
Pacific Northwest Field Seminars
Questers
Sierra Club
Society Expeditions
Sobex Expeditions
Student Conservation Association
Trans-Pacific Tours
University Research Expeditions Program
USDA Forest Service
Wild Horizons Expeditions
Wilderness Southeast
Yellowstone Institute
Zoar Outdoors
Zoetic Research

"If children are to keep alive their inborn sense of wonder, they need the companionship of at least one adult who can share it, rediscovering with them the joy, mystery and excitement of the world we live in."

Rachel Carson

60 Eco-Vacations

Organizations

The organizations listed alphabetically in this section from *Alaska Discovery* to *Zoetic Research* have been chosen to represent a wide range of choices. Every organization completed a questionnaire, answered inquiries, and sent program materials and up-to-date information. These organizations are experienced, reliable, and active in environmental vacations, and answer their mail and phones.

Travel is always an unpredictable business, as those who work in it know only too well. Situations change from day to day, and even from minute to minute. Every effort has been made to ensure the accuracy of the information in this book, but contact the organization to confirm the details before making a decision.

62 Eco-Vacations

Alaska Discovery

369 South Franklin Street
Juneau AK 99801
Phone: (907)586-1911
Fax: (907)586-2332
Contact: Office

Since 1972, Alaska Discovery's team of highly qualified wilderness guides has taken thousands of people into spectacular settings throughout Alaska by canoe, sea kayak, raft, and backpack.

The company's programs have won recognition from the Alaska State Legislature for "pioneering environmentally sound use of the Alaskan wilderness," and for providing "absolute minimum impact on flora and fauna combined with maximum visitor appreciation."

On each trip, participants learn efficient wilderness living techniques and low impact camping. Groups are generally limited to 10 people. Participants help with camping and cooking chores. People of all ages and backgrounds can enjoy the trips, but some camping and

Organizations 63

hiking experience in the backcountry is essential to prepare you for roughing it in the remote wilderness.

The company believes that: "More people living in and visiting Alaska should be able to have extended wilderness experiences so that they may know firsthand Alaska's national park and forests; and that, having developed a personal feeling for these areas, each person in his or her own way will strive to protect the natural beauty of America's wilderness areas."

Visiting Admiralty Island you'll see brown bears and eagles in July and August. You can paddle among thousands of silver and pink salmon migrating upstream on a canoe trip on the Tongass River. Or there's a five-day exploration of the Glacier Bay Shoreline, to spot whales, sea lions, porpoise, and sea otters.

Age range: 20 to 65.
Children over 14 are welcome.

Qualifications: Excellent health essential for traveling in backcountry, plus experience tent camping and hiking. Good physical condition on boat trips.

Price range: $950 to $2,200. Some family discounts.

Price includes: Guide services, floatplane, boat charters, expedition equipment, tents, meals.

Participants provide: Personal items.

64 Eco-Vacations

American Cetacean Society

PO Box 2639
San Pedro CA 90731-0943
Phone: (213)548-6279
Fax: (213)548-6950
Contact: Tia Collins

The American Cetacean Society was founded in 1967 and is the oldest whale protection group in the world. Believing that the best way to protect the world's whales and dolphins is to educate the public about them, ACS organizes week-long trips to view whales, dolphins, and sea lions in their natural habitat.

You can go to Mexico's San Ignancio Lagoon aboard a sportfishing boat and observe hundreds of gray whales as well as sealions, elephant seals, and sea birds, or look for finback and blue whales in the Sea of Cortez in Mexico.

ACS groups travel to British Columbia, Canada to observe killer whales, and fly to Australia to visit

Platypus Bay, an annual gathering site for migrating humpback whales.

The ACS publishes a quarterly journal, *Whalewatcher*, and has designed a *Gray Whale Teaching Kit* and *Whale Fact Pack*. The organization's representative in Washington DC, attends International Whaling Commission meetings, and serves as a liaison with other wildlife organizations. The ACS also maintains a library, supports research, and holds conferences.

Age range: 10 to 82.
   Children aged 10 and over are welcome.
Qualifications: None.
Price range: $1,150 to $2,590 plus membership, $25 Active/$500 Patron.
Price includes: Berth aboard ship, meals, leader, tours.
Participants provide: Personal items.

66 Eco-Vacations

American Hiking Society

**1015 31st Street NW
Washington DC 20007
Phone: (703)385-3252
Fax: (703)754-9008
Contact: Susan Henley**

The American Hiking Society was created in 1977 to protect the interests of hikers. Its Volunteer Vacations program sends teams around the country to help build and maintain America's trails and pathways.

Trail workers bring their own sleeping bags and tents. Most work sites are in remote primitive areas so volunteers must be in good physical condition and able to backpack and camp out.

AHS publishes an annual booklet, *Helping Out in the Outdoors*, that lists hundreds of volunteer jobs and internships available. You can be a campground host in the Nez Perce National Forest in Idaho, where you provide information, and lead nature walks. If you have

Organizations 67

an interest in history, you can volunteer at Tennessee's Shiloh National Military Park. Or you can take your skills in photography and carpentry and offer to help in the 2,500-acre Palisades Interstate Park in New Jersey.

The AHS also works on federal legislation, and confers with the National Park Service, Bureau of Land Management, and US Forest Service to draw attention to hiking trails. Since 1940, more than 40,000 miles of trails in America's parks and public lands have disappeared and since 1969, the number of hikers has more than doubled.

Age range: 16 and up.
Children are welcome on some projects.
Qualifications: Varies depending on project.
Price range: $30 registration fee for Volunteer Vacations. *Helping Out* booklet costs $5.
Price includes: Information packet, food, tools, safety equipment, supervision on site.
Participants provide: Sleeping bag, tent, personal items.

> *"For 32 hours of work a week, I was offered free housing and laundry facilities just two and a half miles from the office. They also offered giant sand dunes, berry and mushroom picking, hiking, boating, crabbing, clamming, fishing."*
> Retired woman, campground host.

68 Eco-Vacations

American Horticultural Society

7931 East Boulevard Drive
Alexandria VA 22308
Phone: (800)777-7931/(703)768-5700
Fax: (703)765-6032
Contact:
  Frank Robinson/Executive Director
  Liz Smith/Special Events.

At its headquarters at River Farm, Virginia, the American Horticultural Society offers internships and volunteer programs. River Farm has a dwarf fruit tree orchard, a water garden, a wildflower meadow, and an extensive rose garden, and also presents displays by different plant societies. Internships run for several months, individually designed for each student. Volunteers can help for as long as they want.

The AHS also arranges tours that focus on the plant world. You can visit the gardens surrounding the historic mansions from New Orleans to Memphis as you travel down the Mississippi on a riverboat.

Organizations 69

You can take a tour of the alpine meadows of the Colorado and the arid plains of the Southwest. And there's a tour of the English countryside and traditional gardens in the Cotswolds and Kent.

A cruise along the northern coast of the Mediterranean explores magnificent private and public gardens in France, Italy, Yugoslavia, and Greece. A fall program visits famous gardens in Japan, China, and Thailand.

The Society, founded in 1922, also offers a Gardener's Information service and supports amateur and professional horticulturists throughout the country.

Age range: 30 to 80.
Children under 18 welcome if accompanied by parent.

Qualifications: None

Price range: $3,000 to $4,000. A donation to AHS is included in the price of all tours.

Price includes: Transportation, lodging, specified meals, guide.

Participants provide: Personal items.

70 Eco-Vacations

American Museum of Natural History

Discovery Tours
Central Park West at 79th Street
New York NY 10024-5192
Phone: (800)462-8687/(212)769-5700
Fax: (212)769-5755
Contact: Dick Houghton

Discovery Tours have long been concerned with conservation, environmental issues and preservation of the ecology. Founded in 1950, the Museum tours now visit dozens of places around the world. Trips are led by experts who give lectures, slide shows, videos, and movies to enrich the travel experience. Most trips are aboard cruise ships.

A special 1991 tour to Hawaii takes travelers to see the last total eclipse of the sun visible from the United States until 2017, paddles along the dramatic cliffs of the Na Pali coast aboard rubber rafts, and treks through Volcanoes National Park and Haleakala Volcano.

Organizations 71

In Africa, the program combines a luxury tenting tour of Tanzania to see the migration of the wildebeest and zebra in Serengeti National Park with a visit to the endangered mountain gorillas in Rwanda's Parc National des Volcans. Leaders include Penelope Bodry-Sanders, biographer of Carl Ethan Akeley whose efforts led to the establishment of the first mountain gorilla sanctuary, and Peter Jones, an archaeologist who worked with Mary Leakey.

In Europe, there's a tour of Ice Age paintings in northern Spain and southwestern France led by Dr. Ian Tattersall, chairman and curator of the Museum's Department of Anthropology.

A tour of New Zealand is accompanied by five experts who share their knowledge of anthropology, geology, ornithology, marine biology, and ocean environments as participants follow the route of Captain James Cook, explorer of the glaciers and marine life of South Island.

Age range: 10 to 90.
Children over 12 accepted on lecture programs.
Qualifications: None. Some trips require walking over rough terrain, or strenuous exertion.
Price range: $2,000 to $3,000 for land programs: $4,000 to $10,000 for cruises. These include membership in the Museum.
Price includes: Everything except airfares.
Participants provide: International airfare.

American Wilderness Experience

PO Box 1486
Boulder CO 80306
Phone: (800)444-0099
Fax: (303)494-2996
Contact: Dave Wiggins

AWE! will plant a tree for every participant in one of their backcountry trips this year, in cooperation with the American Forestry Association's Global Releaf Program. And you'll get complementary membership in the American Forestry Association, the nation's oldest citizen conservation group, "our way to thank you while helping our precious forestlands," as company president Dave Wiggins explains.

American Wilderness Experience, founded in 1971, operates as a clearing house for year-round travel adventures. Its catalogs list trips in the United States, Hawaii, Peru, Mexico, and New Zealand, offered by experienced travel companies.

Organizations 73

You can choose to stay at a dude ranch and experience cowboy life, join a deluxe snowmobile tour of Yellowstone Park, try a llama trek in Colorado with llamas to carry the baggage so you can enjoy the views, or experience a wellness workshop in the Florida Keys where you dance with dolphins.

Other trips take you backpacking through Canyonlands National Park to see desert bighorn, puma, coyote and golden eagle, or on exciting whitewater rafting, canoeing, horsepacking, and camping trips.

AWE! provides detailed itineraries, books trips and airlines reservations and provides all inclusive travel packages.

Age range: 20 to 80.
    Children over 8 are welcome.
Qualifications: No prior experience required.
Price range: $75 to $125 per day per person.
Price includes: Meals, camp equipment, special equipment (horses, rafts, llamas, etc.), guides, some transportation.
Participants provide: Sleeping bags, pad, personal items. Rental equipment available.

co-Vacations

American Youth Hostels

Discovery Tours/Dept 860
PO Box 37613
Washington DC 20013-7613
Phone: (202)783-6161
Contact: Program & Education Dept.

Low-cost biking and hiking trips for those who are young in spirit are offered in the United States and in Europe by AYH, now in its 57th year of operation. Travelers often stay in AYH hostels, which are dormitory-style lodgings with bunk beds with mattress, pillow, and blanket. You provide the sheet sleeping sack.

"All AYH Discovery Tours emphasize responsible tourism with awareness of and respect for natural environments," notes an organizer. "AYH Tour leaders are trained in low-impact travel techniques and practice the principle of treading lightly on our environment."

Bike or hike tours run for a week to a month or more. There's a 44-day exploration of Europe, a 38-day bike

Organizations 75

trip along the Pacific coast, a 22-day tour of the Greek Islands, a 15-day bike trip through French Canada, and a week's trail work in California's John Muir Wilderness Area.

Trips are designed for teens (15 to 18), young adults (17 to 25), adults (18+), and mature adults (50+). Groups have no more than nine participants plus an AYH-trained leader, and are geared to different levels of ability.

Age range: 15 to 90.
Children over 15 are welcome.
Qualifications: Membership in AYH at $25 a year for an adult. Applicants must be in good physical condition and able to meet the demands of the tour, and must provide a health report completed by a physician.
Price range: $250 to $1500.
Price includes: Lodging in AYH hostels or camping facilities, camping equipment, group-prepared meals, transportation, group activities budget, leadership.
Participants provide: Sheet sleeping sack.

Appalachian Mountain Club

PO Box 298
Gorham NH 03581
Phone: (603) 466-2721
Fax: (603)466-2822
Contact: Reuben Rajala

When you hike along a trail, have you ever wondered who cleared the rocks, painted the markers along the way, and built bridges across the streams?

The Appalachian Mountain Club, founded in 1876, is the oldest and largest recreation and conservation organization, and knows all about trail restoration and preservation.

Members volunteer to cut back overgrown bushes, repair shelters, and clear fallen trees. AMC members spend thousands of hours a year clearing more than 1,200 miles of trails in the Northeast, including sections of the Appalachian Trail.

Organizations 77

The AMC works in cooperation with the National Park Service, US Forest Service, other organizations and landowners on projects. Its guide, *Trail Building and Maintenance*, is recognized nationally.

You can join a one-week volunteer base camp and work on trail restoration in New York's Catskill Mountains, Mount Greylock in the Berkshires of Massachusetts, or the White Mountains in New Hampshire. Weekend projects are available.

In New Hampshire, the AMC runs the White Mountain Hut System and Pinkham Notch Camp, as well as several camps in New England.

AMC also provides crews for service projects in Alaska's Chugach National Forest, Wyoming's Grand Teton National Park, Maine's Acadia National Park, and the US Virgin Islands' National Park.

Age range: 14 to 60 +. Average age: 18-40.
Children under 18 welcome.
Qualifications: Good health and some backpacking experience. Training in the use of hand-tools, safety procedures, and maintenance techniques provided.
Price range: $25 to $150.
Price includes: Room and board, leaders, tools, some equipment.
Participants provide: Work clothes, personal items.

78 Eco-Vacations

Arctic Odysseys

Special Interestours
3430 Evergreen Point Road
PO Box 37
Medina WA 98039
Phone: (206)455-1960
Fax: (206)454-6287
Contact: Skip Voorhees

There are three North Poles. There's the Magnetic Pole, defined as an area of magnetic attraction caused by a glob of iron "floating" around in the earth's magma, which attracts compasses. Located off the southeast coast of King Christian Island, the Magnetic Pole moves, and causes the "variation" on maps which must be constantly updated.

The Geographic North Pole is the top of the world, the place where the meridians meet at 90 degrees north latitude. And the Geo-magnetic North Pole is where the lines of the earth's magnetic field converge, on the northwest coast of Greenland, north of the US Air Base at Thule.

Organizations 79

Arctic Odysseys will visit the Geo-magnetic Pole for the first time in 1991 by plane. The route follows Robert Peary's Columbia Meridian Route along the 70th meridian from Cape Columbia on Ellesmere Island to the Pole. Looking down on the polar ice camp, participants will understand something of the obstacles facing those who have attempted the surface route to the pole. A landing on the ice at the pole is planned with time to plant flags.

The company was founded in 1976 by Skip and Susan Voorhees, and Susan was the first woman to lead a group to the North Pole. They also offer dog sled trips to Baffin Island; a stay in Cape Dorset to see the Aurora Borealis; a boat trip on Wager Bay to observe the polar bears in their natural habitat; and a visit to an Inuit archaeological restoration and arts workshop.

Age range: Adult.
   Children under 18 are not usually accepted.
Qualifications: These trips appeal to those with an interest in wildlife, ornithology, photography, local cultures.
Price range: $2,800 to $8,490.
Price includes: All air, ground and water transportation, meals, accommodations, from start of Odyssey.
Participants provide: Airfare to starting point, meals, hotels, passports, personal items.

80 Eco-Vacations

Arctic Treks

Box 73452E
Fairbanks AK 99707
Phone: (907)455-6502
Contact: Carol Kasza & Jim Campbell

"Late to bed and late to rise,
Lets one enjoy the midnight skies."

That's the best advice for visitors who come to Alaska's Brooks Range in the summer.

The sun is up for 24 hours. At midnight a golden glow fills the sky. Migrating birds nest among the wild flowers on the tundra, grizzlies forage with their cubs, and moose browse in the willows. You'll see Dall sheep, eagles, snowy owls, musk ox, lynx, and wolverines in this untouched landscape.

Arctic Treks leads trips to Mt. Doonerak, the highest peak in the Central Brooks Range, to the headwaters of the Noatak River, and into the High Arctic region, all wilderness areas far from civilization.

Organizations 81

You'll hike up mountains without trails, float down rivers where fish abound, camp by streams where animals unafraid of humans come to drink. On one trip, you see the migration of thousands of caribou streaming south from the Brooks Range.

"Our focus now is on saving the Arctic National Wildlife Refuge from oil development," says Carol Kasza of Arctic Treks, former instructor for Colorado Outward Bound School, and past president of the Alaska Wilderness Guides Association. "When people experience the true wilderness and magnificent beauty of this part of the world, it becomes unthinkable to destroy it."

Age range: Teenagers to 70s.
   Children under 18 welcome if in good physical shape and experienced backpackers.
Qualifications: While the hiking pace is moderate, the land is rugged and has no trails. Backpacking trips will be more enjoyable for those in good shape and who are experienced backpackers. The river floats range from true float trips to those with some moderate whitewater. Each person will be part of the paddle crew in their raft.
Price range: $1,975 to $2,300.
Price includes: Roundtrip airfares from Fairbanks, Alaska, all meals, group equipment, guide service.
Participants provide: Personal items.

82 Eco-Vacations

Arizona Raft Adventures

4050 E. Huntington Drive
Flagstaff AZ 86004
Phone: (800)786-RAFT/(602)526-8200
Fax: (602)526-8246
Contact: Cathy Fenton

AzRA specializes in raft trips through the Grand Canyon. The company's president, Robert Elliott, devotes half his time to environmental issues related to preserving the Grand Canyon.

Elliott is the primary spokesperson for the river recreation community, working to alert the public to the damage caused by the Glen Canyon dam operations on the beaches and ecosystem in the Grand Canyon. A percentage of the profit from trips is given to conservation groups helping to protect the Grand Canyon.

Every summer AzRA boatmen raft through the Grand Canyon using oar, paddle, and motor boats. Some trips offer special programs on astronomy, wilderness medicine, and on the geology, botany, climate, and environment of the Grand Canyon. Other AzRA trips raft Idaho's Salmon River, Utah's San Juan River, and rivers in Baja California and Costa Rica.

The company supports Project RAFT, Russians and Americans For Teamwork, created to establish rafting exchanges between the United States and the Soviet Union to promote world peace through rafting.

Age range: 10 to 80.
Children over 10 are welcome.

Qualifications: People of varying physical ability and with no river or camp experience take trips.

Price range: $900 to $1,700.

Price includes: Transportation from Flagstaff, all meals, beverages, life jackets, waterproof bags, travel connections, AzRA mug, river guidebook.

Participants provide: Eating utensils, alcoholic beverages, soda, personal gear, transportation to Arizona, hotel for day before and after trip, camping equipment (rentals available).

"Nothing can compare with rafting through rapids, swimming under waterfalls, sleeping under the stars, and waking with the sun. All I want to do is do it again." A participant.

84 Eco-Vacations

Arizona State Parks

800 W Washington/Suite 415
Phoenix AZ 85997
Phone: (602)542-4174
Fax: (602)542-4180
Contact: Richard Evans, Jr.

To protect the riches of Arizona's numerous prehistoric and historic archaeological resources, the state has initiated a Site Steward Program to provide trained volunteers to watch archaeological sites. Participants attend four hours of classroom work and four hours of field training, and are then sent out to monitor the condition of selected archaeological sites and areas.

"The remains of our cultural heritage are continually threatened by artifact hunters and vandals who illegally destroy or take for their own personal profit these irreplaceable resources that belong to all Americans," notes Jack Bashaw, State Program Coordinator.

Site stewards are needed in many of Arizona's 27 state parks and sites. Also, volunteers are recruited to serve as campground and interpretive hosts. Campground hosts are on hand to greet visitors, help them get settled, answer questions and give out publications. Interpretive hosts explain park rules and regulations, and provide activities and programs for visitors.

All positions demand a four-week minimum stay, and are available year-round. Volunteers may live near the park or camp at a free campsite.

Age range: Over 18.
   Children are not accepted.
Qualifications: Description of positions sent on request.
Price range: Free campsite provided.
Participants provide: Food, transportation, accommodations.

86 Eco-Vacations

Backroads Bicycle Touring

**1516 5th Street
Berkeley CA 94710
Phone: (800)245-3874
Fax: (415)527-1444
Contact: Elizabeth Gignilliat**

The bicycle is a healthy vehicle. There's no pollution, and no gas guzzling. You provide the power and the exercise is good for you. So you can take a vacation on a bicycle with a clear ecological conscience.

Backroads Bicycle Touring has been perfecting its bike trips since 1979. You don't have to be a jock; trips are geared to all levels of expertise.

There's a 16-day tour of China staying at inns; an 8-day tour of France staying at inns; and weekend camping in Point Reyes in California. Other trips travel to Oregon, Idaho, North Carolina, New Mexico, Louisiana, Maine, Vermont, England, Bali, Thailand, New Zealand, Hawaii, Australia, and Italy.

BBT's 70-page award-winning catalog describes the routes in detail and gives frank assessments of every trip, such as: *"Beginner may need to shuttle part of 4th day,"* or *"Mostly level and gradual grades, one 2,000 foot climb,"* or *"Beginners can enjoy this tour by shuttling certain stretches."*

A staff member notes: "There's never any hurry. Our basic route can normally be cycled in three to five hours. Those wanting to cycle more challenging routes can follow our longer options. Those wishing only short distances or easy routes can hop in the van and be shuttled."

Age range: All welcome. Most people are 35 to 55.
  Children under 18 are welcome, and there are student trips for 14 to 18.
Qualifications: Just an interest in bicycling.
Price range: $185 to $2,897.
Price includes: Accommodations, most meals, two tour leaders, maps and directions given to guests each day, use of support van during tour. Bike and equipment rentals available. Free bike helmets.
Participants provide: Bicycle, personal items.

88 Eco-Vacations

Baja Expeditions

2625 Garnet Avenue
San Diego CA 92109
Phone: (619)581-3311
Fax: (619)581-6542
Contact: Stuart Scott

The Forgotten Peninsula of Baja is a region of stark desert beauty surrounded by ocean. Since 1974, Baja Expeditions has been offering whale-watching cruises, sea kayak expeditions, scuba diving programs, and mountain bike excursions in this unique environment.

You can take a week's cruise in one of the company's two boats, where naturalist guides and an extensive library provide all the information you need about the finback, blue, minke, and humpback whales who migrate to these warm waters in the winter months. From the boat, you take skiffs to secluded islands along the way to observe sealions and seabirds.

For the active, there are week-long kayak trips into Magdalena Bay, the Sea of Cortez and around Espiritu Santo Island to see the huge gray whales. Here participants camp out on sandy beaches under the stars and eat freshly caught fish.

To view the landscape of Baja, take a mountain bike tour explores the hidden corners of the peninsula where there's virtually no traffic. From a base camp in the National Park of the Sierra Juarez mountains of northern Baja, bikers take trips to lakes, abandoned mines, and working cattle ranches of the inland region.

Age range: Adults.
  Children under 18 not usually accepted.
Qualifications: None. Costa Rica trip needs paddling experience.
Price range: $450 to $1,975.
Price includes: Land arrangements, accommodations, meals, beverages, hotels in itinerary, and most related trip equipment. Airfare to La Paz included from Los Angeles, Tucson, or Tijuana.

90 Eco-Vacations

California State Polytechnic University

3801 West Temple Avenue
Pomona CA 91768-3342
Phone: (714)869-4051/4045
Contact: Laszlo Szijj/Jonathan Baskin

Two professors of biology lead an exploration of the ecology of Venezuela to find indigenous plants and wildlife of this tropical zone.

Venezuela includes almost every variety of tropical landscape. Participants will spend three days among the coral reefs along the Caribbean coastline, and snorkel in ocean waters relatively unaffected by pollution. There are tours of small coral islands with groves of coconut palms and mangrove thickets where thousands of herons, pelicans, and frigate birds nest.

The group visits the Central Plains region, a flat, grassy landscape, with many rivers and forests and an astonishing variety of wading birds, including storks, ibises, herons, egrets and many species of ducks and geese.

Hawks and macaws are often seen. It's hoped to spot monkeys, ocelots, anteaters and capybaras too.

In the high Andes area, participants will hike in the cloud forests around Merida, and look for flowering epiphytes, plants that live on air. There will also be a cablecar ride to the top of Pico Bolivar in the Andes at 16,000 feet to explore a glacier and snowfield.

Age range: 18 and up.
   Children under 18 not accepted.
Qualifications: None.
Price range: About $3,000 for 22-day trip.
Price includes: Air fare, transportation, accommodations, meals, instruction, guides.
Participants provide: Personal items.

92 Eco-Vacations

Camp Denali & North Face Lodge

PO Box 67
Denali National Park AK 99755
Phone: Summer: (907)683-2290
Winter: (603)675-2248
Fax: Summer: (907)683-2290
Winter: (907)675-9125
Contact: Wallace or Jerryne Cole

If you spend a few days in the heart of this wilderness area, you will experience a land almost untouched by human beings. You can hike in flowering alpine meadows, see the active glaciers that edge the mountains, watch shorebirds and waterfowl in the myriad of ponds along the roads, or spot caribou, moose, or grizzly bears in spruce forest or on tundra hillsides.

There's canoeing on Wonder Lake, rafting down Moose Creek, fishing for Arctic Greyling or Mackinaw Trout. You can go goldpanning in the nearby historic Kantishna mining district, and flightseeing for an aerial view of the peaks of the Alaska Range.

Camp Denali and North Face Lodge are wilderness lodges located in the center of the Denali National Park where nature, not man, dominates. The park stretches for 5.7 million acres including the permanently snow-covered Alaska Range. Both lodges face a spectacular view of Mount McKinley, the highest mountain in North America.

Staff naturalists provide information during outings and give evening programs on the flora, fauna, and history of the area.

Age range: All ages.
   Children under 18 are welcome.
Qualifications: None.
Price range: $195 per person per day.
Price includes: Transportation, all meals, lodging, guiding, use of recreational equipment, natural history interpretation.
Participants provide: Personal items.

94 Eco-Vacations

Canoe Country Escapes

194 South Franklin Street
Denver CO 80209
Phone: (303)722-6482
Contact: Brooke or Eric Durland

Traveling through the wilderness of lakes and forests in a canoe is the ideal way to explore the natural beauty of the Minnesota-Ontario Boundary Waters. The canoe's design is little changed from the birch bark canoes of the Ojibway Indians and the French-Canadian trappers as they paddled across Minnesota's lakes centuries ago.

Canoe Country Escapes has been leading groups on trips through this region since 1980. They explore the thousands of square miles of Canada's Quetico Provincial Park adjoining the equally large Boundary Waters Canoe Area Wilderness in Superior National Forest.

You'll find jewel-like lakes ringed by rock ledges, white birch and Norway pine, brilliant sunsets, nightly loon serenades, and spectacular displays of the Northern Lights. You can stay at lodges or camp out.

Special family trips introduce children to the delights of canoeing in the wilderness, picking blueberries for lunch, swimming in the clear waters, learning how to fish and set up camp, and shivering at ghost stories round the fire.

Brooke and Eric Durland, who met on a trip, offer two-day, five-day, and 10-day excursions. They share the rich history of the region with the groups, and explain the effects of acid rain in the area to emphasize the need for environmental protection.

Age range: 4 to 80.
   Children over four welcome on Family Trips.
Qualifications: None.
Price range: $325 to $775.
Price includes: Canoe instruction, guide services, all meals and equipment, ground transportation to remote put-in points, optional airport pickup in Duluth, and dinner, lodging and breakfast the nights before and after trips.
Participants provide: Personal items.

96 Eco-Vacations

Canyonlands Field Institute

**PO Box 68
Moab UT 84532
Phone: (801)259-7750
Contact: Sue Bellagamba**

CFI encourages people to learn about the natural and cultural heritage of the Colorado Plateau, a region which stretches across the Four Corners region of Utah, Colorado, Arizona and New Mexico. The Institute is associated with Bates Wilson and his ranch near Moab, Utah. Wilson, now retired, was the first superintendent of Canyonlands and helped it gain National Park status.

Through field hikes and outdoor exploration, CFI introduces participants to Arches and Canyonlands National Parks, the La Sal and Abajo Mountains, and the valleys of the Colorado and Green Rivers.

Some seminars take place on canoe and river-rafting trips to see special areas of the landscape, which is rich in geologic features, unusual plants, and animals. There

Organizations 97

is an abundance of prehistoric Indian rock art panels and ruins.

You can sign up for one-day, weekend, or week-long seminars to learn about endangered fish, the future of the desert bighorn sheep, photography in the canyons, the pattern of the night sky, desert wildflowers, and archaeology among other topics. CFI also offers several Elderhostel programs.

Age range: 10 to 80.
   Children are welcome on certain programs.
Qualifications: None.
Price range: $35 to $400. Optional $15 membership.
Price includes: Varies; usually instruction, camping, some meals.
Participants provide: Depends on program.

98 Eco-Vacations

Center for Responsible Tourism

PO Box 827
San Anselmo CA 94979
Phone: (415) 258-6594
Contact: Virginia Hadsell

"I founded the center in 1984 because I had been listening to people in the developing world who were talking so much about what was happening to them, their land, their culture, their beaches, and no one was listening," explains Virginia Hadsell.

The North American Coordinating Center for Responsible Tourism aims to change the attitudes and practices of North American travelers and persuade them to be part of the struggle for justice in tourism in the Third World.

It coordinates the North American Network (NANET), made up of groups who join with the Ecumenical Coalition of Third World Tourism in Bangkok to fight against economic, cultural, and environmental exploit-

Organizations 99

ation of Third World people by mass tourism. The Center encourages alternative tourism which will benefit both residents and travelers, where local people have a voice in tourism development and receive an equitable share of the benefits.

It publishes the NACCRT *Code of Ethics for Travelers*, a quarterly newsletter, and acts as a clearing house for books, articles, videotapes and slide shows on Third World countries. Its *Directory of Third World Travel Alternatives* lists accommodations and services that benefit local economies.

If you send a small donation and a self-addressed stamped envelope, the Center provides a list of questions to ask tour operators, cruise line personnel, and travel industry professionals on Third World issues.

Age range: 18 to 80.
>Children under 18 are welcome to join.

Qualifications: Concern for people and environment at the other end of the airplane ride.

Price range: Varies.

Participants provide: Donations and support.

100 Eco-Vacations

Clearwater Inc

112 Market Street
Poughkeepsie NY 12601
Phone: (914)454-7673
Contact: Director

The *Clearwater* is a classic Hudson River 106-foot sloop which was launched in May 1969 to dramatize the plight of the polluted Hudson River in New York. The sailing boat travels to towns and cities along the river alerting residents to environmental problems.

Each year, thousands of school children and adults take a trip on the *Clearwater* to explore the natural history and ecology of this great waterway. They hoist the sails and steer the boat, examine fish and water samples, and absorb the views of water and land around them.

Volunteers are welcome as crew members on the boat, or to help with environmental efforts to save the Hudson River.

Members monitor compliance with industrial pollution along the river and assist local communities fight development proposals and polluting waste disposal projects along the river.

The member-supported organization was created in 1966 and is also active in environmental lobbying in Albany, NY and in Washington DC, and in court cases related to PCB removal programs.

Age range; Any age.
   Children are welcome.
Qualifications: None.
Price range: Varies. Membership information available.
Participants provide: Personal items.

"Everybody wake up!
Open your eyes! Stand up!
Be children of the light
Strong, swift, and sure of foot.
Hurry, clouds,
From the four quarters of the universe.
All hearts be glad!"

From a Pueblo song.

102 Eco-Vacations

Colorado Trail Foundation

548 Pine Song Trail
Golden CO 80401
Phone: (303)526-0809
Contact: Gudy Gaskill

Creating and maintaining 500 miles of Colorado hiking trails is a demanding job. But dedicated volunteers do the work, and spend hundreds of hours on these challenging trails that climb mountains, cross streams, pass through wilderness areas, and traverse state and national forests. Keeping the trails in good condition has been the work of the Foundation since 1976.

Volunteers sign up for a week of trail work, from Saturday to Saturday, though they can stay longer if they want. Participants camp in Colorado's National Forests near trail sites, and share all the cooking and camp chores.

The work involves constructing new sections of the trail, repairing bridges, and clearing and rebuilding older sections. This can include moving rocks out of the way, rerouting a section of the trail, cutting back trees and branches, taking away fallen treetrunks, and removing debris.

"People come without a friend and leave with many," comments Gudy Gaskill. "Many people write to me about the satisfaction of giving something back after years of using the trails."

Age range: 16 to 85.
Children under 18 welcome if accompanied by a responsible adult.
Qualifications: Need to be able to do physical work.
Price range: Free.
Price includes: All food, tools, hard hats, base camp equipment.
Participants provide: Work clothes, personal items.

104 Eco-Vacations

Cornell's Adult University

626 Thurston Avenue
Ithaca NY 14850
Phone: (607)255-6260
Fax: (607)255-7533
Contact: Ralph Janis

CAU offers summer on-campus seminars and year-round travel education programs on a range of environmental and ecological topics, led by Cornell's finest scholars and teachers.

There's a geological exploration of the mountains of New Mexico that includes visits to cliff dwellings and ancient ruins of the Anasazi culture. Seminars on marine biology and ecology are offered at the Shoals Marine Laboratory on Appledore Island in the Gulf of Maine.

A seminar in Maryland studies the culture and ecology of Chesapeake Bay, and is led by a specialist in marine biology and ichthyology.

In Florida, participants explore Big Cypress National Preserve, the Fahkahatachee Strand where the rare Florida panther lives, and the waterways of Everglades National Park with its shore birds and manatees.

Upcoming tours will travel to New Zealand's North and South Islands to study their unique ecology and natural history.

Programs on-campus in Ithaca include field seminars in botany, geology, entomology, and paleobiology. There are separate activities for children of all ages.

Age range: 35 to 70.
 Children welcome on some programs.
Qualifications: None.
Price range: $600 to $3,500.
Price includes: Accommodations, most meals, entrance fees, field trips, academic program.
Participants provide: Personal items.

106 Eco-Vacations

Crow Canyon Archaeological Center

23390 County Road K
Cortez CO 81321
Phone: (800)422-8975/(303)565-8975
Fax: (303)565-4859
Contact: Lynn Dyer

Why did thousands of Anasazi Indians abandon their homes in a beautiful canyon and mesa at the end of the 13th century? What caused them to leave a place where they had set up their farms, built stone houses, and established their lives?

Those are the questions archaeologists at Crow Canyon are trying to answer. They created the first Division of Environmental Archaeology in 1990 to consider the theory that environmental changes forced the people to leave the region.

It's part of the long-term study of the region led by Dr. Karen Adams and Dr. Mark Hovezak. They hope to combine elements of archaeology and botany to provide

Organizations 107

a unique cross-disciplinary understanding of the relationships between ancient humans and their natural world.

Crow Canyon offers programs year-round for adults and students who want to learn more about the American Southwest, and workshops for teachers on bringing archaeology into the classroom.

There are also programs for school groups and high school students. One high school student commented: "Crow Canyon was awesome. I learned more in five days than a year of anthropology."

Volunteers live in a lodge or in four-bed hogans, attend lectures, and help archaeologists on projects. These include assisting with the retrieval, identification, and interpretation of plant, animal, and human remains, and learning to analyze tree rings, pollen cores, and changes in the shape of the landscape over time.

Age range: High school students and adults.
> Children are welcome for school programs, or during Family Week.

Qualifications: None

Price range: $400 to $1600.

Price includes: Meals, lodging, tuition, program costs, and transportation from Cortez, Colorado.

Participants provide: Transportation to Cortez.

108 Eco-Vacations

Earthwatch Expeditions

**PO Box 403N
680 Mount Auburn Street
Watertown MA 02272-9104
Phone: (617)926-8200
Fax: (617)926-8532
Contact: Blue Magruder/Lisa Montesi**

Earthwatch was founded in 1971 to focus attention on research into the environment. Today, Earthwatch is in the forefront of environmental organizations. The organization aims to improve human understanding of the planet, the diversity of its inhabitants, and the processes that affect the quality of life on earth.

Each year, Earthwatch sends 3,000 volunteers to work with scientists worldwide. Opportunities to help are listed in the Earthwatch catalog. In Fairbanks, Alaska, Dr. Daniel Jaffe, for example, is trying to identify the components of Alaska's increasing smog and nitrogen oxide levels and monitor their seasonal cycle; he needs

Organizations 109

hardy wilderness hikers and skiers to collect and analyze pollutant samples from the air and snow.

In Alice Springs, Australia, Dr. Aharon Arakel wonders whether the dead lakes in the region can teach us about water management; his volunteers walk through the desert terrain surveying playa lakes, noting landforms, collecting sediment and water samples from trenches, and helping to analyze the water samples.

Earthwatch provides *Briefings* on projects for $25, which can be put toward the expedition cost. These detailed descriptions provide the history of the project, its research mission, background of investigators and staff, goals, field logistics, reference maps, in-country information, and a bibliography of reading materials.

Age range: 16 to 84.
Children over 16 are welcome.

Qualifications: Enthusiasm.

Price range: $700 to $2,100.

Price includes: Accommodations, food, research staff and equipment, instrumentation, briefings, expedition vehicles.

Participants provide: Travel to site, side trips, personal items.

"It's an unparalleled way to keep on growing and learning." A participant.

110 Eco-Vacations

Eco-Tourism International

Forum International
91 Gregory Lane #21
Pleasant Hill CA 94523
Phone: (415)671-2900
Fax: (415)946-1500
Contact: Dr. Nicholas Hetzer

Eco-Tourism International and Forum Travel International are the travel departments of Forum International, which is dedicated to creating "a world-wide forum for education, research, and action on a transdisciplinary, supra-national and ecosystemic basis."

Founded in 1956, it describes itself as the oldest and largest Eco-Tourism group in North America. Over the years, the company has organized more than 1,200 tours and expeditions to explore nature, culture, and people, with special emphasis on environmental integrity, social responsibility, human health and fitness.

Organizations 111

You can take one- to two-week trips to the Amazon rainforests, Central America, the Galapagos Islands, Antarctica, Southern Africa, the Sahara. Participants can also join research projects in Northern California and Oregon, among others. All programs emphasize:

1. Minimum environmental impact.
2. Minimum impact on, and maximum respect for, host cultures.
3. Maximum economic benefits to host country grass roots.
4. Maximum 're-creational' satisfaction to participating tourist.

The company does not publish a catalog but provides information about specific programs on request.

Age range: 7 to 100.
Children under 18 are welcome.
Qualifications: None.
Price range: $55 a day, and upwards.
Price includes: Transportations, accommodations, meals, leadership, guiding, documents.
Participants provide: Personal items.

112 Eco-Vacations

Eye of the Whale

P.O.Box 1269
Kapa'au HI 96755
Phone: (800)657-7730/(808)889-0227
Fax: (808)889-0227
Contact: Mark & Beth Goodoni

> *"If I could have my way about it, I would go back there and remain the rest of my days. It is paradise. When you are in that blessed retreat, you are safe from the turmoil of life."*

That was how Mark Twain felt after visiting Hawaii in 1873. You can experience the original natural beauty of the traditional untouched Hawaii of the last century with Mark and Beth Goodoni. They specialize in taking small groups to see the real Hawaii.

Between January and March, they offer five-day whalewatching and sailing trips to explore the west coast of the Big Island between Kawaihae and Kealakekua Bay. The trip includes work for an ongoing research project for the North Gulf Oceanic Society, so they will be photo-identifying individual humpback whales, recording their mating songs, and collecting base line data. You'll see the spectacular aerial displays and intricate behaviors of the humpback, and also watch the bottlenose, spinner, and spotted dolphins along with pilot and false killer whales.

At night the boat drops anchor in a secluded bay where you can swim, snorkel, and enjoy the sunset.

Other Hawaii trips take you to Volcanoes National park to walk across the crater of the world's most active volcano; to hike the cliffs of the Na Pali coast; along the trails of Kokee State Park to identify native flowers and trees; and visit what was once a leper colony on Molokai.

Age range: 13 to 72.
 Children under 18 are welcome.
Qualifications: None.
Price range: $135 a day.
Price includes: All lodging, meals (except a couple of dinners), inter-island airfares on trip, sailing, ground transportation, activities, naturalist guide.
Participants provide: Airfare to Hawaii, personal items.

114 Eco-Vacations

Florida Oceanographic Society

890 N E Ocean Boulevard
Stuart FL 34996
Phone: (407)225-0505
Fax: (407)225-4725
Contact: Gary Guertin

Nature expeditions with members of the Florida Ocean-ographic Society explore the beaches of South Hutchin-son Island, and cruise the Indian River lagoon in the St. Lucie Inlet, near the Indian River Plantation Resort. Both trips introduce visitors to the history and marine life of the area.

The Society was created in 1964 to increase knowledge and understanding of Florida's ocean and coastal environment through education and research. The Society supports many research projects, and studies of nearshore reefs, and surveys of water quality. It oper-ates a computerized 24-hour Coastal Weather Infor-mation Service, and publishes a pamphlet on *Safe Boating through the St. Lucie Inlet.*

Future plans include developing a Coastal Science Center with regional aquariums, marine research laboratories, library, marine exhibits, conference center, wildlife refuge areas, nature trails, and sea turtle and mammal rehabilitation centers.

Age range: 18 to 88.
Children under 18 are welcome on some projects.
Qualifications: None.
Price range: Depends on project. Membership; $30 individual.
Participants provide: Depends on project.

116 Eco-Vacations

Florida State Parks

Division of Parks and Recreation
3900 Commonwealth Blvd/MS 525
Tallahassee FL 32399
Phone: (904)488-8243
Contact: Park Volunteer Coordinator

Florida has more than 400,000 acres of parks, recreation areas, and wilderness, which offer a unique view of tropical beauty and environmental tranquility.

You can canoe in the protected areas of Blackwater River, explore the sandpine forest of Rocky Bayou, or swim in the waters of Ponce de Leon springs. Or you can spot black skimmers, snowy plovers, and other shore birds on a coast barrier island.

Historical tours take you to earth temple mounds of an ancient Indian burial site by Lake Jackson, and to visit the oldest plantation house in Florida where cotton, black-eyed peas and sugar cane were once farmed.

There are more than 100 state parks, and close to 15 million people visit them every year. Camp hosts and park volunteers are welcome to help preserve Florida's park. Campground hosts stay for six to 12 weeks, while volunteers can choose a more flexible schedule.

Volunteers greet visitors, conduct early morning bird walks, assist rangers in picking up trash, and answer campers' questions. They also help with special activities including native American festivals, traditional craft workshops, sea turtle searches, and stargazing seminars. The parks operate year-round, and a free guide is available.

Age range: Adults
   Children under 18 are not accepted.
Qualifications: Adaptability, interest in nature and people.
Price range: Free.
Price includes: Campsite for campground hosts.
Participants provide: Camp gear, food, personal items.

118 Eco-Vacations

Food First Institute

Good Life Study Tours
145 Ninth Street
San Francisco CA 94103
Phone: (415)864-8555
Fax: (415)864-3909
Contact: William M. Alexander

Spend a month living in Kerala in southern India with families of a cooperative community who "live lightly on the land."

Kerala is a hot, sultry, coastal region with high humidity. Its per capita income is lower than all Indian averages. Yet in contrast to the poverty, the people enjoy education and health at levels close to those in the west. Birth rates are low and declining. There is 78 percent adult literacy, nearly double that of the rest of India. Life expectancy is 68 years, compared to 57 years in the rest of India.

The Institute's Good Life Study Tours, which began in 1989, place participants in local homes for a month to experience a different way of life. There is only primi-

Organizations 119

tive bathing and toilet facilities but host families provide boiled drinking water. Beds are usually made of wood with a small pad, not a mattress. Meals are eaten with the family, and are usually a plate of rice with flavorings from a choice of side dishes.

Every participant is accompanied by a full-time translator and cultural guide, and attends seminars three times a week. It's a unique experience of sharing life in a community where people balance their daily needs for food and shelter without exploiting the environment.

Director William Alexander notes: "We offer an opportunity for Americans to educate themselves by complete immersion in a good life which can survive in a world of more people and less resources."

Age range: 18 to 90.
There are no programs for children as yet.
Qualifications: Fluency in English. Mature demeanor, experience of living independently as in camping, experience of a culture other than your own.
Price range: $900 for 30-day program, $1,600 for a couple.
Price includes: Room, board, transportation and tips from Trivandrum, translator, cultural guide, program services.
Participant provides: Airfare from US to India.

120 Eco-Vacations

Foundation for Field Research

P.O.Box 2010
Alpine CA 91903
Phone: (619)445-9264
Contact: Thomas Banks

The Foundation brings together enthusiastic volunteers with scientists who need assistance on their projects. Since 1982, it has coordinated scores of year-round environmental research expeditions world-wide. Projects are chosen after careful investigation, which includes on-site visits, proposals sent out for peer review, and research into the scientist's background. Volunteers complete a detailed questionnaire and are placed where their skills match project needs.

In the United States, volunteers can join a study of the rock art in the canyons of Lake Havasu City, Arizona, or help with research into prairie dog colonies in Montana. Another program searches for fossil and dinosaur remains in New Mexico's San Juan Basin.

Organizations 121

On the Caribbean island of Grenada, volunteers can work with an anthropologist filming the dancing, costumes, and celebrations of the annual carnival in August, or they can assist an archaeologist who needs scuba divers to help retrieve artifacts from a 1650 village under water.

In Europe, volunteers excavate a castle in Wales while assisting on a survey of the preservation of Welsh names. In West Africa, they can join a survey of southern Sierra Leone villages, or study tool use among chimpanzees.

In Mexico, volunteers help draw, photograph, and measure the mansions of a once-thriving town in the silver mine region. They can travel into the cloud forests of Chiapas to study the nesting habits of the brilliantly plumed Quetzal bird. Or they patrol the beaches at night to save the eggs of giant leatherback turtles.

Age range: 14 to 86.
Children under 18 are welcome.
Qualifications: A willingness to work.
Price range: $395 to $1,485.
Price includes: Contribution to scientific project, lodging, food, field manager/cook, ground transportation.
Participants provide: Travel to site, personal items.

122 Eco-Vacations

Gerhard's Bicycle Odysseys

PO Box 757
Portland OR 97297
Phone: (503)223-2402
Fax: (503)223-5901
Contact: Gerhard Meng

Non-polluting bicycle tours through Switzerland, Austria, Italy, and Norway are offered by Gerhard Meng, who established his company in 1974 and personally leads the tours. Groups are limited to 20 adults. Travelers stay at quality hotels, country inns, or castles with first-class food.

Gerhard carefully selects routes along country lanes with little traffic, away from the normal tourist areas. Daily distances are short, avoiding hills whenever possible. More strenuous routes are available for the advanced cyclist. Each rider is given detailed maps and route outlines and is able to set his or her own pace.

The support vehicle carries the luggage, is available for mechanical problems, and can provide a lift if you're tired.

Age range: 18 and over.
Children accepted if accompanied by a parent or guardian.
Qualifications: Physically and mentally fit, and young at heart.
Price range: $1,995 to $2,595 for 14 days.
Price includes: Hotels, most meals, transportation, sightseeing, daily outline, map, tips, taxes, leaders, pre-departure packet.
Participants provide: Airfare, bicycle, helmets, personal items.

"To experience the heartbeat of a country from a bicycle has made me feel a part of it rather than a mere visitor."   A participant.

124 Eco-Vacations

Global Exchange Reality Tours

2141 Mission Street #202
San Francisco CA 94110
Phone: (415)255-7296
Contact: Tour Coordinator

Global Exchange was founded in 1988 to help advance the internationalist movement. Its Reality Tours are special travel programs that introduce people from the United States to those in the Third World. Programs have toured the rainforests in Brazil, the villages of the Philippines, and communities in Appalachia and the townships of South Africa among others.

On the tour, participants meet farmers, members of grassroots environmental movements, religious leaders, women's groups, and unions. They also visit hospitals, schools and villages, and spend time with people in their homes.

This non-profit organization offers an annual family trip in Mexico for parents and children, with child care and

Organizations 125

special children's activities provided. Special itineraries are available for groups; a Michigan university professor took his class of students to El Salvador and Nicaragua to illustrate the course he was teaching.

One graduate student who toured Mozambique and Zimbabwe commented: "The trip was amazing! It allowed me to do things I never would have done on my own. I especially appreciated the high level contacts with government officials."

Age range: Adults.
Children under 16 do not usually apply, except for family trips with parents.

Qualifications: Anyone with a genuine interest in learning about the regions visited. Participants should be flexible and sensitive to Third World realities.

Price range: $500 to $3,300, depending on region. Membership: $25 donation.

Price includes: Roundtrip airfare from gate city (Miami or New York), food, lodging, preparation materials, organizing costs, transportation. A limited number of scholarships are available.

Participants provide: Travel to gateway city. Personal items.

126 Eco-Vacations

Habitat for Humanity International

**121 Habitat Street
Americus GA 31709-3498
Phone: (912)924-6935
Fax: (912)924-6541
Contact: Global Village Coordinator**

Habitat for Humanity's Global Village program sends volunteers to construct homes in developing nations. Participants work together with the local residents in building a Habitat project, and spend from one to three weeks in the country.

"All workcampers work side by side with their international brothers and sisters. They live, eat, work and play just as the local nationals do," explains Frank Stoffle, program coordinator.

Habitat for Humanity, founded in 1976 by Millard and Linda Fuller, is an ecumenical Christian housing ministry that aims to provide housing for poor people and end homelessness around the world. Habitat has built more than 10,000 homes worldwide, and works through both local affiliates and international projects in close to 35 countries. The houses are built using volunteer labor and donated materials, and sold at no profit, with no interest charged over a long-term mortgage.

Families are chosen by local selection committees on the basis of need and ability to repay the mortgage, and their willingness to become part of the Habitat for Humanity partnership.

Age range: 18 to 90.
Children under 18 not accepted.
Qualifications: None.
Price range: Varies. Average is $2,000-$3,000.
Price includes: Transportation, food, lodging, materials, orientation.
Participants provide: Spending money, insurance.

International Bicycle Fund

4887 Columbia Drive South
Seattle WA 98108-1919
Phone: (206)628-9314
Fax: (206)628-9314
Contact: David Mozer

"We encourage alternatives to motor vehicles," explains David Mozer, who went to Africa as a Peace Corps volunteer, and has traveled there extensively. "Our travel programs are culturally sensitive, environment friendly, and economically beneficial."

The International Bicycle Fund is a non-profit organization that assists economic development projects utilizing bicycles, sponsors educational bicycle travel programs to Kenya, Zimbabwe, Cameroon, West Africa, and Tunisia, and publishes travel materials including a Code of Responsible Travel, and books about bicycling in Africa.

Organizations 129

IBF tours present an intimate view of the African continent. Participants are expected to encounter different customs, attitudes, and living standards with an open and tolerant mind. Daily cycling distances range from 20 to 60 miles, and the emphasis is on enjoying Africa and seeing places seldom visited by tourists.

In Zimbabwe, cyclists set out from the city of Harare, bike to the eastern highlands to visit development projects and cultural sights, visit Inyanga National Park, rural areas, and botanical gardens, tour the Odzi and Sabi River Valleys, and return to Harare. In Kenya, cyclists travel from Nairobi to the Masai Mara National Park for a van safari, visit the spectacular Rift Valley, Lake Baringo, and cross the western highlands to Lake Victoria, returning by train to Nairobi.

Age range: 18 to 74.
No children.
Qualifications: Good health and cycling ability.
Price range: $990 to $1,290.
Price includes: Accommodations, two meals a day, transfers, park fees and museums, guides, excursions.
Participants provide: Airfare to Africa, incidental expenses.

130 Eco-Vacations

International Bicycle Tours

7 Champlin Square
PO Box 754
Essex CT 06426
Phone: (203)767-7005
Fax: (203)767-3090
Contact: Frank Behrendt

Try a non-polluting easy bicycle tour of England, the Netherlands, Belgium, Germany, and France, or a fall tour of Cape Cod in Massachusetts. Led by Frank Behrendt, who grew up in Amsterdam, International Bicycle Tours reflect his knowledge of Europe and the United States.

Multi-lingual guides greet you at the airport and remain with the group. You stay in comfortable inns and friendly, small hotels. And the pace on the nine-day trips is leisurely, with plenty of stops for taking pictures, munching on snacks, or just relaxing.

In England, you bike through the East Anglian countryside, where John Constable painted his landscapes, and visit picturesque harbors, ancient churches, and Norman cathedrals, and take your meals in local pubs.

Choose among several tours of the Netherlands, including a spring ride through the dazzling tulip fields in bloom, and a Fifty Plus tour for those who haven't ridden a bicycle in years. A bike tour through France visits the Loire valley with its magnificent chateaux and fields of sunflowers.

Age range: 6 to 84.
Children under 18 welcome if accompanied by parents.
Qualifications: Ability to bicycle.
Price range: $1,200 to $1,600. $375 for Cape Cod four-day trip.
Price includes: Accommodations, breakfast and dinner daily, tips and taxes. Bike rentals available.
Participants provide: Personal items, own bicycle.

132 Eco-Vacations

International Expeditions

One Environs Parks
Helena AL 35080
Phone: (205)428-1700
Fax: (205)428-1714
Contact: Veronica Rhoads

For many years, International Expeditions has conducted natural history travel programs to tropical rain forest areas. In addition to tours in Peru, it offers programs in Belize, Costa Rica, and the jungles of Ecuador.

Concern about the continuing destruction of tropical rain forests led the company to hold an International Rainforest Workshop in Peru, with seminars on different aspects of rainforest life and how best to preserve them. Funds from the workshop will be used for the Amazon Center for Environmental Education and Research, to be built on part of a primary rain forest in the Explornapa Rain Forest Reserve in Peru. This will serve as an environmental education base and study area for researchers to share their knowledge and experience with visitors.

The company also offers nature tours to close to 30 destinations worldwide. You can visit a national park in Venezuela to see the flamingoes, ibis, and frigate birds. You can tour Alaska and observe sea otters, puffin, seals, and whales. You can join safaris in Africa to see its unique wildlife.

Age range: 20 to 80.
   Children under 18 are sometimes accepted.
Qualifications: None.
Price range: $699 to $5,112.
Price includes: Airfare from gateway city, transportation, accommodations, most meals, naturalist guides, excursions, activities.
Participants provide: Transportation to gateway city, passport, tips, personal items.

134 Eco-Vacations

International Research Expeditions

140 University Drive
Menlo Park CA 94025
Phone: (415)323-4228
Contact: Director

IRE invites volunteers to assist scientists in the field with research projects in animal behavior, ornithology, marine biology, archaeology, ecology, and zoology.

Research teams are small, usually no more than ten people, and field conditions vary from first class hotels to modest local homes to tent camps in remote areas.

You can study the appetite of elephants, the alarm calls of the red-backed hawk, the minke whales of the Pacific Northwest, Uaraki monkeys in Peru with their red facial coloring and short tails, octopus in the Caribbean, Brazilian leaf-cutting ants, and Australian tiger snakes.

In Argentina you learn how to develop techniques to capture rainwater using windmills and underwater pumps in order to provide residents with adequate water supplies.

Programs in archaeology include excavating metal working sites in Namibia, Africa to discover the cultural heritage of the people who lived there in 500 BC. In the Grand Canyon, backpack along three trails to visit prehistoric sites and collect baseline information on conditions for the Park Service.

Age range: Adults.
   Children under 18 not usually accepted.
Qualifications: Interest and enthusiasm.
Price range: $425 to $1,750 contribution, tax-deductible.
Price includes: Transportation from staging area, shared food and accommodations, camping/field gear, research equipment and supplies, orientation materials.
Participants provide: Transportation from home to staging area, personal expenses, passports, visas.

136 Eco-Vacations

International Zoological Expeditions

210 Washington Street
Sherborn MA 01770
Phone: (508)655-1461
Contact: Fred Dodd

From December through August, IZE offers birding, natural history, and wildlife tours in Belize, a small country south of Mexico on the Caribbean, and about the size of Massachusetts.

Known as British Honduras until it gained independence in 1981, Belize has a population of 150,000, and the official language is English. It also includes one of the last untouched tropical rain forests, magnificent coral reefs, sunlit cays with colorful fish, winding rivers, pine-covered grasslands, and lowland marshes.

IZE has spent 20 years developing study and research tours of the ecology of the country. From its field stations in the remote primary rain forests and on the barrier reef, tours visit wildlife sanctuaries, and snorkel and dive in the Caribbean. Visitors look for river turtles, giant iguanas, crocodiles, and howler monkeys. Orchids and bromeliads in full flower grow in abundance. And the bird population includes large keel-billed toucans, brilliant scarlet macaws, red-footed boobies, and boat-billed herons, as well as parrots, hummingbirds, woodcreepers, and colorful tanagers.

IZE also has cottages for rent on South Water Cape, one of the islands of Belize.

Age range: 6 to 90.
    Children under 18 are welcome.
Qualifications: None.
Price range: $400 to $1,000.
Price includes: Charter air, boats, guides, lodges, hotels, buses, all meals.
Participants provide: Personal items.

138 Eco-Vacations

Journeys

3516 NE 155th
Seattle WA 98155
Phone: (800)345-4453/(206)365-0686
Fax: (206)363-6615
Contact: Kurt Kutay

"We want to hear you went for the scenery, the nature, or the culture, and your returned with an unexpected appreciation of other peoples and a fresh perspective on life at home,"explains a staff member.

Journeys was created in 1977 to introduce people to remote areas of the world as a voyage of personal discovery. Later, Journeys established the Earth Preservation Fund to identify and support village and community level projects which promote environmental or cultural preservation.

Staff members, travelers, local officials and residents work together on projects. These include trash removal and maintenance along the much-traveled Inca trails in Peru; tree-planting in the Himalayas where tourists over-use scarce fuelwood for cooking and heating; and

Organizations 139

restoration of village prayer wheels and monasteries in Ladakh, Nepal.

You can join an EPF project and contribute your efforts to the work. You can also take a Journeys expedition to the Himalayas, China, Tibet, India, Thailand, New Guinea, South America, Alaska, and Hawaii among other places.

On an African safari you tour wildlife reservations and also meet the Maasai and other tribes in East Africa. In Japan, a cultural exploration takes travelers by train to the Tohoku region to stay in Japanese inns, sleep on futons, see zen temples, and trek in the rugged countryside. And the Annapurna Family Trek in Nepal visits local families along the way.

Age range: 6 to 75.
Children under 18 welcome on family trips.
Qualifications: Good physical health. Trips arc graded Easy, Moderate, Strenuous, or Very Strenuous depending on amount of hiking and camping.
Price range: $995 to $3,250.
Price includes: Ground transportation, accommodations, most meals, naturalist guide, driver, airport transfers.
Participants provide: Airfare, personal items, some meals.

La Sabranenque

217 High Park Boulevard
Buffalo NY 14226
Phone: (716)836-8698
Contact: Jacqueline C. Simon

La Sabranenque, established in 1969, restores medieval villages, buildings, and rural sites in Europe. The non-profit association invites volunteers to work on restoration for a few weeks in the summer in France or Italy.

Its first project, near Avignon in southern France, was to restore the village of Saint Victor la Coste, which dates back to the 11th century. Abandoned in the 1900s, the village was in ruins when the work began. Volunteers cleared vegetation and rubble, and restored each house individually, using local materials and traditional techniques.

The success of that effort led to invitations to restore other ancient buildings in nearby villages. In 1988, the organization was honored with two awards for its work in the restoration of Romanesque chapels in France.

Organizations 141

All programs include a training and preparation session in Saint Victor La Coste. The work includes stone masonry, stone-cutting for window and door openings, carpentry for ceilings and roofs, floor and roof tiling, path paving, and dry stone walling among other projects.

"I enjoyed the work environment and the communal atmosphere as much as the unique opportunity of discovering the history and culture of the Provencal region in a whole different perspective," commented an American participant.

At least one day each session is spent touring the region, and participants are welcome to take trips in their free time. Volunteers come from a variety of backgrounds, professions, and nationalities.

Age range: 18 to 65.
   Children under 18 not accepted.
Qualifications: None. Some knowledge of French or Italian helpful but not necessary.
Price range: $490 for a two-week project.
Price includes: Shared furnished room, full board, all activities, at least one excursion.
Participants provide: Airfare to France.

142 Eco-Vacations

Lisle Fellowship

433 West Sterns Road
Temperance MI 48182-9509
Phone: (800)477-1538/(313)847-7126
Fax: (419)537-7719
Contact: Dr. Mark B. Kinney

The Lisle Fellowship organizes seminars for mature people interested in personal growth within a group setting.

Founded in 1936, and one of the oldest intercultural educational programs in the United States, the seminars are designed to bring together people from diverse backgrounds to share a learning experience and discover greater tolerance for different ideas.

Two seminars are held abroad. In Mexico, there is a seminar on *Art and Culture: Artisans and Community Development*. In Indonesia, the focus is on *Modernization in Paradise; Encounters of the Human Kind*.

At the University of Toledo, Ohio, a summer Elderhostel program and an open seminar will be held examining different aspects of intercultural experience including the experiences of foreign students.

The Fellowship programs are organized by Dr. Mark B. Kinney, president of the Board of Directors.

Age range: Adults over 18.
    Children under 18 accepted with program leader's permission.
Qualifications: None.
Price range: $999 to $2,600/$270 for Elderhostel.
Price includes: Airfare from Los Angeles, transportation, meals, accommodation, seminars, leaders.
Participants provide: Transportation from home.

144 Eco-Vacations

Lost Coast Llama Caravans

77321 Usal Road
Whitethorn CA 95489
No Phone
Contact: Nancy Peregrine

Friendly llamas carry your camping gear while you walk through the breath-taking scenery of the Sinkyone Wilderness State Park and King Range Conservation area in California.

Llamas are sturdy independent animals whose feet cause far less trail damage than do horses or mules. Llamas carry heavy loads with ease and are used to mountain trekking. They're usually friendly to humans.

This company designs individual trips for groups who want to travel with llamas in July and August on three- or four-day excursions. You decide when you'd like to go and for how long, and write to the company with your choices.

Be prepared to hike up to six miles a day because llamas don't carry people on their backs. All trips follow environmentally sound camping and hiking practices.

Age range: All ages.
 Children are welcome.
Qualifications: Ability to walk 3 to 6 hours a day.
Price range: $75 per day per person; min. 6 people.
Price includes: Food, guides, equipment, llamas.
Participants provide: Sleeping bag, pad, personal gear, optional tent.

"For my part, I travel not to go anywhere but to go. I travel for travel's sake. The great affair is to move."
Robert Louis Stevenson

Marine Sciences Under Sails

PO Box 3994
Hollywood FL 33023
Phone: (305)983-7015
Contact: Joanne Bowie/Jan Smith

With hands-on get-wet programs, MSUS provides outdoor education for people of all ages about the life and history of the sea around Florida.

You can take short trips on a sailing boat in the Florida Keys to experience first-hand how the early pioneers explored the region and lived with the sea. There are also one and two-week study-cruises to the Caribbean islands to explore coral reef ecology, sea birds, ocean holes, mangrove ecology, and sandy beaches and shoals. The courses include instruction in sailing.

MSUS organizes day hikes into Florida state parks to learn about the native and exotic plants of the area, with a special study of mangrove trees. You can visit the John Pennekamp Coral Reef State Park, take glassbottom boat trips to an outer coral reef, canoe in the mangroves, and snorkel. Or you can visit the Everglades and examine a freshwater slough, a pine and palmetto trail, and a hardwood hammock trail.

"When students get directly involved in a natural environment, they appreciate it more. They become emotionally involved. They see it being taken away from them by man's misuse, and they fight to defend it," says MSUS founder Ned Webster.

MSUS also provides in-school Marine Science programs bringing marine animals and plants into the classrooms.

Age range: All ages.
   Children are definitely welcome.
Qualifications: Some age restrictions on some programs.
Price range: $3.50 to $150.
Price includes: Instruction, overnight stays, meals (varies with program).
Participants provide: Depends on program.

148 Eco-Vacations

Massachusetts Audubon Society

Natural History Travel
South Great Road
Lincoln MA 01773
Phone: (800)289-9504
(617)259-9500 Ext 7410/7411
Contact: Susan Moody/Travel

Walking for miles along beaches at night without a flashlight looking for turtles crawling up the sand to lay their eggs is a major environmental focus of this group. MAS sends volunteers to work with scientists to observe and protect the Leatherback and Green Sea Turtles of Costa Rica. Programs last for 10 or 17 days.

Supervised by the Caribbean Conservation Corporation, one project examines leatherbacks (who can grow to 1,200 lbs) and measures the effects of temperature on nesting behavior as well as on heat flow and oxygen consumption.

Another study looks at the huge fleets of green turtles who return every summer to Tortuguero to lay their eggs in the black sand beach. Since 1954, volunteers have assisted the CCC in a long-term study to monitor the beaches at night, tag nesting sea turtles, and record data about them.

The Society also offers natural history tours to Alaska, the Galapagos, the Amazon, Antarctica, China, and other places. These trips emphasize conservation of nature and culture, and are led by experienced naturalists and local guides.

Age range: Turtle research project, 14 to 74; Tours, 30 to 70.
Children under 18 are not usually accepted.

Qualifications: Interest, and general good health.

Price range: $1,422 to $1,876 for turtle research; $1,590 to $7,000 for tours.

Price includes: RT airfare from Miami (gateway city for tours), transportation, accommodations, meals, instruction, portages, services, taxes.

Participants provide: Airfare to gateway city, personal items. A physician's certificate may be required for turtle research.

"The project is ideal for those who want working 'hands-on' experience, and you leave knowing that you have contributed to something worthwhile."   A participant

150 Eco-Vacations

Mobility International USA

**P.O.Box 3551
Eugene OR 97403
Phone: (503)343-1284 (Voice and TDD)
Contact: Susan Sygall/Executive Director**

MIUSA is dedicated to integrating persons with disabilities into international and exchange programs with the motto "Challenge yourself and change the world."

Members can:
- live and study in other countries with a host family;
- join international workcamps;
- attend travel workshops for people with disabilities;
- share information about disabilities with people from other countries.

Participants have traveled to Costa Rica, Germany, Italy, China, and England. Travelers include people who are blind, deaf, use a wheelchair, have cerebral palsy, or other disabilities.

Organizations 151

One member on a dialysis machine noted: "I learned that ocean cruises and river rafting are possible." And a blind member wrote: "I traveled and stayed with families all over Europe."

Mobility publishes a guidebook to international educational exchanges for people with disabilities, a quarterly newsletter, a manual on how to organize programs, and two videotapes; *Looking Back, Looking Forward* with comments from people with disabilities who have traveled abroad; and *Mi Casa Es Su Casa* where volunteer exchange students from the US and Costa Rica improve services for those with disabilities.

In 1991 there's a four-week Environmental Youth Exchange Program between Russia and America for people with or without disabilities.

Age range: 16 and older.
Children under 18 can be members.
Qualifications: None.
Price range: Varies with grants budget. Soviet trip: $2,500. Membership fee: $20.
Price includes: RT airfare, transportations, accommodations, all meals, activities, cultural programs.
Participants provide: Personal items.

152 Eco-Vacations

Mountain Travel

6420 Fairmount Avenue
El Cerrito CA 94530
Phone: (800)227-2384
Fax: (415)525-7710
Contact: Dena Bartolome

Mountain Travel has been offering minimum-impact adventure trips since 1967, led by knowledgeable and concerned guides who understand the importance of environmental preservation.

Recently, the company established The Mountain Travel Fund for the Environment, a program where a percentage of income from each trip goes to protect and improve part of the environment where the trip took place. In the past, Mountain Travel promoted the establishment of the Sagarmatha National Park in the Khumbu region of Nepal, and the Machu Picchu National Park in Peru.

In Africa, you can trek in Kenya and Tanzania, take a walking safari in the Selous Game Reserve, visit Namibia and Zimbabwe. In the Himalayas, you can climb the spectacular mountains around Annapurna, Everest, Kanchenjunga, and Kashmir. There's a camel safari in India, a tour of the Silk Road from China to Pakistan, and an elephant safari in Thailand.

In Europe, there are inn-to-inn hikes through the Alps in Switzerland or the Pyrenees in Spain, and treks in Poland or Czechoslovakia. Other tours explore Bali, Indonesia, Australia, Hawaii, Ecuador, Patagonia, Guatemala, Costa Rica, and more. The company also organizes special seminars for doctors on medicine in the wilderness, mountains, and tropical forests.

Age range: Most travelers are 30 to 60.
Children under 18 are welcome.
Qualifications: Some apply on particular trips.
Price range: $890 to $6,000.
Price includes: In camp: all meals, porters, pack animals, guides, cooks, ground transport, camping, commissary equipment. In cities: hotels with private bath where available, airport transfers on group flights, porters, sightseeing, entrance fees, leadership, local guides, permits. Group airfares available.
Participants provide: Visa fees, most meals in cities, tips, insurance, excess baggage charges, beverages, medical costs, personal items.

154 Eco-Vacations

National Audubon Society

950 Third Avenue
New York NY 10022
Phone: (212)832-3200
Fax: (212)593-6254
Contact: Margaret Mullaly Carnright

Tours with the Society are designed for its members through Special Expeditions. They are usually cruises to places with fascinating natural scenery, plant, bird and animal life.

You can travel along the Norwegian coast beyond the Arctic Circle to explore legendary fjords. The region is home to vast colonies of seabirds, and also to polar bears, reindeer, and giant tusked walruses. The program is led by Jean Porter, Director of Operations at the Audubon's National Environmental Education Center in Connecticut.

You can cruise amid the windswept islands off the coast of Scotland and Ireland. You'll see archaeological dis-

Organizations 155

coveries dating back to the Stone Age, seabird colonies with more than 70,000 birds, and Shetland ponies less than four feet high.

In Oregon, you follow the route 19th century explorers Lewis and Clark took up the Columbia River, and travel through the Columbia River Gorge, the locks of Bonneville Dam, and Hells Canyon, the deepest gorge in North America.

The Society's concern about the environment and the impact of tourism led to the creation of its *Travel Ethic for Environmentally Responsible Travel*, to which all its tour operators must adhere, and which is reprinted in the Appendix, page 225.

Age range: Adults 21 to 91.
    Children over 12 welcome on some trips.
Qualifications: Membership/$30 a year.
Price range: Cruise costs vary, depending on cabin chosen.
Price includes: Accommodations, meals, transfers, excursions, sightseeing, guides, tips and taxes, reading lists.
Participants provide: Airfare, transportation.

156 Eco-Vacations

National Society for Internships and Experiential Education

3509 Haworth Drive/Suite 207
Raleigh NC 27609-7229
Phone: (919)787-3263
Contact: Director

If you'd like to be an intern in national parks, wilderness areas, and cities, you'll find more than 2,000 environmental internship opportunities available in NSIEE's National Directory of Internships.

The Directory describes internships around the country where you work on land preservation, archaeology, air pollution, and water preservation among others, plus details of the organizations offering them, who is eligible, and how to apply. Indexes to fields of interest, particular regions, and organizations are included.

Founded in 1971, NSIEE brings together people and institutions interested in experiential education to provide a grassroots exchange of information. As well as the Directory, NSIEE publishes *A Guide to Environmental Internships* to show environmental organizations how to utilize internships effectively; a three-volume resource book on *Combining Service and Learning*; and a study of internships in the humanities.

Age range: High-school to mid-career.
    Children under 18 are accepted in some cases.
Qualifications: Varies, depending on internship.
Price range: Varies. Some internships provide stipends.
Participants provide: Varies.

158 Eco-Vacations

National Wildlife Federation

1400 16th Street NW
Washington DC 20036-2266
Phone: (800)432-6564/(703)790-4363
Fax: (703)442-7332
Contact: Sheri Sykes/Senior Coordinator

Environmental education is the focus of the work of the National Wildlife Federation. Its programs cover a wide range of environmentally related topics and are designed for people of all ages. Its national membership is made up of affiliate organizations in nearly every state and territory.

Every summer NWF offers Conservation Summit seminars to introduce members to the natural world. The week-long seminars are held near national parks or similar settings in Colorado, Vermont, North Carolina, New York, Montana and other places.

The format allows adults and families to design their own schedules from scores of programs offered inclu-

Organizations 159

ding all-day nature hikes, wildlife ecology, hummingbird gardening and classes on how to negotiate for the environment. Evenings offer slide shows, stargazing, square dances, sing-alongs, and other activities.

There are special programs for children. Teen Adventures take 13 to 17 year olds on outdoor hiking and exploration trips. The Junior Naturalist Program provides classes and field trips to encourage school-age children to discover the natural world about them. And a preschool program introduces younger children to simple nature activities.

The NWF also publishes *National Wildlife* and *International Wildlife* magazines for adults and families, *Ranger Rick* and *Big Backyard* for children, and distributes millions of Wildlife Conservation Stamps every year.

Age range: Infants to seniors.
Children are welcome.
Qualifications: Membership in NWF, $16 a year.
Price range: $75 to $225 for week's program: accommodation prices vary, depending on choice of room.
Price includes: Registration for all classes. Accommodation fees include all meals, use of meeting space, grounds, recreation facilities, evening activities.
Participants provide: Transportation, personal items.

160 Eco-Vacations

Natural Habitat Wildlife Adventures

One Sussex Station/Suite 110
Sussex NJ 07461
Phone: (800)543-8917/(201)702-1525
Fax: (201)702-1335
Contact: Carol McKay

Only 25 years ago, baby "whitecoat" seals were clubbed to death on the icefloes of Canada for their fur. But an international protest persuaded the Canadian Government to ban the commercial slaughter of whitecoats in 1987. The market for their white pelts has now disappeared.

In March, you can visit the baby harp seals and their mothers, through the International Fund for Animal Welfare. The animals cover the icefloes in the Gulf of St. Lawrence as they migrate north. Tourism has replaced the income from seal pelts in the region.

Visiting the Gulf of St. Lawrence in early March is like dropping into another world. The sight of hundreds of

Organizations 161

mother seals and their pups is breathtaking. It has to be experienced to be believed. noted one visitor.

In October, this company offers tours to Churchill in Canada for the annual Polar Bear Watch. The bears spend the winter on the pack ice in Northern Canada's Hudson Bay. When the ice melts they are driven to the southern shores for the summer. In October, they begin their migration north. Churchill, known as the Polar Bear Capital of the World, provides a unique view of hundreds of polar bears preparing for their migration.

Tours to Alaska, Africa, and the Galapagos Islands are also available.

Age range: From 8 to 80.
Children are accepted.
Qualifications: None.
Price range: $1,295 to 4,995.
Price includes: Airfares, hotels, meals, transportation, guides, nature and photography presentations, taxes, service charges.
Participants provide: Personal items.

162 Eco-Vacations

Nature Expeditions International

PO Box 11496
Eugene OR 97440
Phone: (800)869-0639/(503)484-6529
Contact: Alan Cameron

In some of the most fascinating regions of the world we study wildlife, environment, people and history, says David Roderick, company founder. Education has always been our first goal, adventure the second.

The company has had a strong commitment to the ideals of ecotourism and specializes in natural history and cultural expeditions around the world since it began in 1973. Trips are led by qualified naturalists, biologists, and local experts, who know where to find the most interesting and unusual places, and respect the cultures of countries they visit.

You can join tours to East Africa, Kenya, and Tanzania. You visit Madagascar, a nearby island with rare and unique plants, animals, and birds, to observe flying

Organizations 163

foxes, leaf-tailed lizards, paradise flycatchers, and several lemur species.

In India, you explore the game sanctuaries of Ranthambore, Bharatphur, and Kanha by elephant, jeep, and on foot. And in Japan you visit Tokyo, Kyoto, Takayama, Nara, climb in the mountain region, and stay in traditional inns.

In South America, you can sail up the Amazon river, explore the fabulous Galapagos Islands that Darwin visited to see the iguanas, sealions, and blue-footed boobies. You can hike to the Inca ruins of Cuzco and Machu Picchu in Peru. Other programs introduce you to Alaskan wildlife, Hawaii's natural history, the ecology of the Pacific Northwest, and the Indian region of Arizona, Colorado, and New Mexico.

Age range: Late 20s to late 70s.
Children under 18 are welcome.
Qualifications: None
Price range: $1,490 to $4,990.
Price includes: Accommodations, transportation, transfers, most meals, sightseeing, local guides, instruction, leadership.
Participants provide: Airfare, passports, visas, alcoholic beverages, insurance, personal items, tips to local guides, boat, or camp crews, airport departure taxes.

164 Eco-Vacations

New York Botanical Garden

Travel Program
Bronx NY 10458-5126
Phone: (212)220-8647
Fax: (212)220-6504
Contact: Carol Gracie

For many years, Carol Gracie and her husband, Scott Mori, curator of tropical plants at the NY Botanical Gardens, have taken small groups to explore the ecology of South America.

Aboard an Amazon river boat, with a local guide who grew up in the region, their program explores Brazil's Rio Negro region.

The group is based in a tropical rainforest where participants collect and process plant specimens, study pollination and seed dispersal, map a new trail, and prepare a natural history guide for it.

"The work is rigorous, but previous volunteer research assistants have shared the thrill of discovering new species, been the first to observe some of the intricate interactions that occur in a tropical rainforest, and marvelled at the diversity and beauty of this vast ecosystem," notes Carol Gracie.

Age range: Adults.
Children under 18 not accepted.
Qualifications: Good physical condition.
Price range: $1,695 to $2,495.
Price includes: Transportation, accommodations, all meals.
Participants provide: Airfare from US, personal items.

166 Eco-Vacations

North Cascades Institute

2105 Highway 20
Sedro Woolley WA 98284
Phone: (206)856-5700
Fax: (206)856-1934
Contact: Saul Weisberg

There are many way to work at saving the world. One of the least glamorous, and most frustrating in the short-term, is education. It is also one of the only ways to effect significant and sustainable change.

This is the credo of the North Cascades Institute, an environmental educational organization, founded in 1985. It offers a range of programs to put people in touch with the natural world of the Pacific Northwest, and works in co-operation with the US Forest Service, the National Park Service, and Western Washington University.

You can take a one-day seminar to observe the winter concentration of bald eagles in Skagit Valley, or a

Organizations 167

weekend to explore bird habitats on the San Juan Islands. You can study mosses and liverworts in the Coronet Bay Environmental Learning Center, learn to distinguish the edible and medicinal plants of the Puget Lowlands, or take a weekend trip on skis to explore the winter ecology of the subalpine and alpine regions in Mt. Baker-Snoqualmie National Forest.

A seminar on endangered species in the Pacific Northwest examines grizzlies, wolves, eagles, spotted owls and animals long associated with the forests of the region, and their relationship to the Endangered Species Act.

There are also three-day field camps for children, backpacking trips into wilderness areas, seminars on the trout and salmon in the waterways, and a houseboat float exploring the Columbia River with an archaeologist.

Age range: 5 to 85.
Children are welcome.
Qualifications: None
Price range: $40 to $500.
Price includes: Instruction, accommodations, sometimes transportation.
Participants provide: Food, transportation if necessary.

168 Eco-Vacations

Oceanic Society Expeditions

Fort Mason Center/Building F
San Francisco CA 94123
Phone: (800)326-7491/(415)441-1106
Fax: (415)474-3395
Contact: Mary Jane Schramm

Oceanic Society Expeditions, a nonprofit group founded in 1972, recently merged with Friends of the Earth to serve as the environmental travel arm of the organization. OES believes that responsibly conducted nature tourism can help save natural areas by providing an income to local communities and an incentive to preserve their wildlife and parks.

A staff member commented: Environmental travel is one very powerful and persuasive way to learn about the earth we need to protect. Education is the vitally important first step.

OES trips are led by professional naturalists. An expedition to see Bahamas dolphins is led by Nancy

Organizations 169

Black, who has conducted research with Pacific white-sided dolphins and harbor porpoises. In Kenya, safaris are led by Tom Lithgow, Jr., born in Tanzania. He is co-founder of a conservation organization that conducts educational wildlife summer camps for school children. Other tours visit Australia, Costa Rica, Belize, Patagonia, the Amazon, Hawaii, and Baja Califormatch.

OES also offers special Nature Watch expeditions where participants assist scientific research on dolphin study in the Bahamas, and whale-watching near Vancouver Island and Alaska.

Age range: 5 and up.
Children under 18 are welcome.
Qualifications: General good health and a sense of adventure.
Price range: $28 (local trips) to $5,000.
Price includes: Accommodations, some group flights and airport transfers, sightseeing, entrance fees, leadership crew, local guides, permits, meals.
Participants provide: Airfare, airport taxes, passports, visas, immunizations, insurance, alcoholic beverages, soft drinks, personal items, medical costs.

"The expedition was terrific! It exceeded my wildest hopes. We saw so many whales we could not count them all." A participant

170 Eco-Vacations

Offshore Sailing School

16731 McGregor Boulevard
Fort Myers FL 33908
Phone: (800)221-4326
Fax: (813)454-1191
Contact: Kirk Williams

The non-polluting sport of sailing is one of the most enjoyable experiences on water, according to those who have tried it.

The Offshore Sailing School promises you will learn to sail after a week's instruction. The curriculum emphasizes preparation, classwork, and hours of hands-on sailing, and more than 70,000 people have qualified for Offshore diplomas.

If you'd like to learn, Steve Colgate, an America's Cup and Olympic sailor, is convinced you can do it. He started his company in 1964 with one boat and one instructor.

Doris Colgate, his wife, is a leader in the women's sailing field. She recently founded the Women's Advisory Board on Sailing, a national group dedicated to increasing the awareness and accessibility of sailing to women.

Sailing courses are offered at Captiva Island, Florida; Tortola, British Virgin Islands; Chatham, Cape Cod; St. Lucia; and at City Island, New York, just outside Manhattan.

Age range: 12 to late 70s.
   Children under 18 are welcome.
Qualifications: None.
Price range: $415 to $2,436.
Price includes: Tuition, accommodations, some meals, welcome party, graduation party, instructional materials.
Participants provide: Some meals, personal items.

172 Eco-Vacations

Overseas Adventure Travel

349 Broadway
Cambridge MA 02139
Phone: (617)876-0533
Fax: (617)876-0455
Contact: Debbie Rosen

A conservation-oriented company since it began in 1979, Overseas Adventure Travel offers scores of programs that contribute directly to the preservation of some of the finest wildlife refuges in the world.

The company was selected as the African Wildlife Foundation's African safari operator, and is the only commercial safari operator on the Advisory Council of the AWF. OAT trips in Africa meet biologists and conservationists to discuss protection for endangered species, including elephants, black rhinos, and cheetahs.

In the Himalayas, OAT has established the Lobuche Conservation Project at Lobuche, the highest campsite along the approach route to Mt. Everest and one of the

Organizations 173

most popular trekking routes. The project involves the construction and maintenance of windproof landfill sites, sanitation facilities for campers, and multi-lingual signs about low-impact travel. On Himalaya treks, OAT uses no wood for cooking; instead, kerosene is carried in to help prevent further deforestation.

The company's illustrated catalog describes its wildlife excursions in Africa; treks in Pakistan, Turkey, Tibet, India and Kashmir; cruises to the Galapagos Islands; and trips to Bali, Borneo, and Hawaii among others.

OAT distributes a *Buyer Beware* brochure warning travelers about illegal wildlife souvenirs. The company donates a percentage of fees to maintain trails and conservation programs in national parks in Nepal, in Machu Picchu in Peru, and to African conservation projects.

Age range: 6 to 85.
　　Children under 18 welcome.
Qualifications: None.
Price range: $1,100 to $3,495.
Price includes: Accommodations, most meals, airport transfers, trip leader, entrance fees, guides, cooks, support staff, pack animals, camp equipment.
Participants pay: Airfares, hotels not in itinerary, drinks, bottled water, alcohol, sleeping bag, tips, passport, immunizations, insurance, personal items.

174 Eco-Vacations

Pacific Northwest Field Seminars

83 South King Street
Seattle WA 98104
Phone: (206)553-2636/7958
Contact: Jean Tobin/Coordinator

This organization is one of 64 non-profit associations around the country that provide interpretive services and programs within the National Park system.

You can join camping, backpacking, walking, photography, sketching, and natural history programs in the parks and forests of Washington and Oregon.

There's a family camping program for single parent and two-parent families to introduce young children to the outdoors. A special barrier-free day in the wilderness is planned for those with disabilities.

Other courses teach the skills of minimum-impact backpacking, study birding in Mount Rainier, observe the night skies, listen for the sounds of wilderness, explore the geology and glaciers of the area, and hike through volcanic landscapes.

All programs are held in the field, and are led by qualified naturalists and guides. On some, there's moderate to strenuous hiking on or off trails while others include strolls along paths.

Age range: People from 25 to 55 usually enroll. Children welcome in some seminars.
Qualifications: None. Participants should be prepared to spend full days outside.
Price range: $25 to $35 per day.
Price includes: Instructors fee and honoraria. Occasionally the cost of a van and a meal.
Participants provide: Transportation, accommodations, food, clothing, equipment.

176 Eco-Vacations

People to People International

501 East Armour Boulevard
Kansas City MO 64109
Phone: (816)531-4701
Contact: Alan M. Warne/VP, Programs

Every year, People to People and the University of Missouri-Kansas City offer issues-oriented traveling seminars for students of all ages interested in expanding their horizons. The organization was founded in 1956 by President Eisenhower.

Two seminars focus on the environment. In Sweden, the program includes meetings with government agencies such as the Swedish Society for the Conservation of Nature, a tour of the world's first online facility to recycle chlorofluorcarbon refrigerants, and discussions about the relationships of human activities to environmental problems. There will also be visits to Uppsala and tours of Stockholm. Participants live with Swedish families.

Organizations 177

In the West Indies, there's a seminar on tropical ecology and field biology at the Springfield Plantation/Archbold Tropical Research Center on the Island of Domenica. Students live in buildings within the 192 acres of the plantation, adjoining a 950-acre tract of pristine tropical rain forest. They work on projects related to the ecology of the region, which has magnificent forests, birds, wildlife, geothermal resources, hot springs, and fumaroles.

People to People also offers seminars on *International Business*, which tours Europe; *International Relations*, held in Budapest and Prague; *Western European Economics*, which travels through Amsterdam, Maastricht, Bonn, Brussels, and Paris; and three seminars on education, drug abuse, and health care in Sweden.

Age range: Adults
Children under 18 not accepted.
Qualifications: Ability to travel independently, use public transportation, join walking tours, carry luggage.
Price range: $1,525 to $2,375.
Price includes: Accommodations in shared room, breakfast, some meals, transportation, entrance fees, group sight-seeing, tuition, educational fees, some health and accident insurance.
Participants provide: Some meals, personal items.

178 Eco-Vacations

Population-Environment Balance

1325 G Street NW/Suite 1003
Washington DC 20005
Phone: (202)879-3000
Fax: (202)879-3019
Contact: Rose M. Hanes

When there were fewer people in the United States, there were fewer environmental problems. America's population continues to grow by some three million every year, concentrated in a few areas. That ever-increasing expansion is a critical threat to cities, and to the water, land, air, and open spaces.

Population-Environment Balance was founded in 1973 as a grassroots member organization committed to stabilizing our population in order to safeguard the carrying capacity of the United States, which means the number of people who can be supported without degrading the physical, cultural, and social environment.

Organizations 179

The organization works to show the American public and policymakers the adverse impact of population growth on America's natural and social environment, and to achieve a national commitment to population stabilization.

Population-Environment Balance runs a number of initiatives related to population. Some current programs include: global warming, family planning, and local growth control. You can join the group for $25 a year, and receive a quarterly newsletter, a quarterly information sheet, and regular fact sheets. The organization welcomes information on local actions or news related to population issues.

Age range: All ages.
Children under 18 are welcome to join.
Qualifications: None.
Price range: Membership, $25.
Participants provide: Varies.

180 Eco-Vacations

Questers

**Worldwide Nature Tours
275 Park Avenue South
New York NY 10010
Phone: (800)468-8668/(212)673-3120
Contact: Frederick Rappaport
Michael Parkin**

Luxury nature tours are the specialty of Questers, founded in 1973. Participants travel first class in groups of no more than 20 people, led by naturalists with a knowledge of the region and its natural ecology.

Questers tours the Hawaiian Islands, Alaska, South Dakota, Wyoming, and Montana. In the Pacific Northwest they visit the Makah Indian Reservation, investigate Mount St. Helens, and look for bear among the glaciers and alpine meadows of Mount Rainier.

In Central America, there are tours in Costa Rica's National Parks and in the Monteverde cloud forest. Other tours fly the length of the Amazon River, walk through the Patagonian grasslands in Chile, visit Angel Falls in Venezuela, and tour Argentina.

In Europe you can explore Iceland, the Highlands of Scotland, Switzerland, Spain, and the Greek Islands where there are enchanting wildflowers, native birds, and volcanoes.

Other tours visit Asia, Africa, Australia, and New Zealand.

Age range: 45 to 65, but all ages are welcome. Children over 15 if accompanied by parents.
Qualifications: Active and in good health.
Price range: $2,280 to $10,683.
Price includes: Airfares, accommodations, all meals, tour director, transportation, sightseeing, tips, taxes, transfers, pre-tour materials.
Participants provide: Insurance, passports, visas, mineral waters, wines, liquors, personal items.

182 Eco-Vacations

Rainbow Adventures

1308 Sherman Avenue
Evanston IL 60201
Phone: (708)864-4570
Fax: (708)864-4597
Contact: Susan Eckert

Outdoor adventures for women over 30 is the specialty of this company founded in 1982, with the emphasis on exploring different environments. The company offers women a chance to travel the world with other women who share similar interests. Trips provide an alternative active vacation choice.

"After years of raising families or working at a career, our women come to us for vacation adventures within an environment that's supportive," notes Susan Eckert, president and founder. She has served in the Peace Corps in West Africa, and is trained in wilderness survival skills.

She offers a horseback riding tour of Ireland along the Killarney Reeks Trail where participants stay in hotels. In the United States, you can cross the prairies in a covered wagon trek and follow the Oregon trail in Wyoming. You can spend a week on a 95-foot schooner sailing in the Caribbean. Or you can choose an exhilarating rafting trip down the Salmon River in Idaho.

Other tours visit New Zealand, safari in Africa, hike into the Grand Canyon, and explore the Nile River in Egypt. All trips are led by expert guides.

Age range: 30 and above.
   No children accepted.
Qualifications: Women over 30, in good health.
Price range: $275 to $4,750.
Price includes: Varies depending on trip.
Participants provide: Personal items.

184 Eco-Vacations

San Jose State University

Office of Continuing Education
San Jose CA 95192-0135
Phone: (408)924-2680
Fax: (408)924-2666
Contact: Sharon Cancilla

Tours and programs related to the environment, ecology, and human relations are offered by the university's Office of Continuing Education.

A 1991 summer tour of the Fiji Islands is led by Gary Klee, professor of geography and environmental studies, who has had extensive experience in research in Micronesia.

The program examines the origins of the islands' land forms and the cultures of the Pacific peoples. It will also study environmental issues related to the conservation of the soil, water, grassland, forest, wildlife, wilderness, and fisheries resources. Participants will be

Organizations 185

able to scuba dive and snorkel along the reefs and atolls, sail along the coast, trek through sugarcane fields, and hike in taro swamps and along tropical wilderness trails.

An unusual seminar in Thailand looks at *American and Thai Cultures and Stress* led by two sociologists from the university, and contrasts the ingredients of the relaxed Thai culture with the feverish pace of American life (subject to local political conditions).

In Kenya and Zimbabwe, you can take a safari odyssey to contrast the history, wildlife, and cultures of the two African countries.

Age range: Adults over 18.
Children under 18 are not generally accepted.

Qualifications: Over 18.

Price range: $2,346 to $4,115.

Price includes: Roundtrip airfare from San Francisco or New York, airport transfers, accommodations, most meals, sightseeing, activities, insurance, information packet, SJSU academic escort.

Participants provide: Tuition fee for credits, additional meals, tips, personal items.

Sierra Club

Outings Department
730 Polk Street
San Francisco CA 94109
Phone: (415)776-2211
Contact: Outings Director

The Sierra Club, an environmental organization founded in 1892, offered its first outing to Yosemite National Park in the summer of 1901.

Today, more than 325 trips are listed in the Outings Catalog, published in the January issue of *Sierra* magazine. Trips are conducted by Sierra volunteer leaders, and you can travel throughout the United States, and to more than 23 foreign countries.

Service trips offer you a chance to preserve some of the most beautiful natural places in the country. In Arizona, you can clear brush and construct waterbars on the Chillicut Trail in the Four Peaks Wilderness, presently a natural research region for observing black bears.

Organizations 187

You can work on trails in Arches Park in Utah, which has exotic plants as well as spectacular views. In Michigan, you repair campsite and portage trails in the virgin forest of the Sylvania Wilderness. In Arkansas, you build a new trail in the Ozarks.

Family outings are designed for parents with young children, to provide a relaxed introduction to camping, hiking, and climbing in the outdoors. These slower-paced trips are offered in Colorado, California, and Mount Desert Island in Maine.

Backpacking and base camp trips hike on trails in Yosemite, the Sierra Nevada, Rocky Mountains in Colorado, Sawtooth Range in Idaho, Wind River Range in Wyoming, and the Cascades in Washington.

Foreign trips explore Africa and visit game preserves and national parks; tour Asia to climb the mountains and experience a camel safari; and visit Europe to walk through England, cycle in Scotland, and hike the Alps.

Age range: All ages.
Children welcome on family trips.
Qualifications: Leader approval is required for most trips.
Price range: $175 to $3,665.
Price includes: Accommodations, food, transportation, guides.
Participants provide: Varies, depending on trip.

188 Eco-Vacations

Smithsonian Research Expeditions

490 L'Enfant Plaza SW/Suite 4210
Washington DC 20560
Phone: (202)287-3210
Fax: (202)287-3244
Contact: Charlene James-Duguid

Pagwa, one of the world's most exciting folk festivals, takes place in Jamaica in March. The celebration focuses on a huge bonfire, called Holika, lit weeks before the event. On the night of the festival, Hindus, Muslims, and Jamaicans of all ethnic origins and religious persuasions walk and dance around the fire to the beating of drums and the singing of Hindu songs. Then as the fire dies down, stories are told, traditional foods served, and songs and folk dances performed until dawn.

Smithsonian associates join two anthropologists studying the celebration. They will collect data to learn more about Jamaica's Indian heritage. Participants conduct interviews, observe events, meet local residents, and

Organizations 189

learn songs and dances. The resulting material will be used in educational programs about Jamaica's cultural heritage.

The Smithsonian Research Expeditions program began in 1988, and offers many opportunities for volunteers. You can help on archival projects at the National Air and Space Museum in Washington DC. You can attend and document the annual Crow Fair in Montana, or help record the annual Loggers Reunion in Idaho.

You can visit the active Arenal volcano in Costa Rica with its erupting ash and lava, search for fossil marine mammals in the Calvert Cliffs which stretch for more than 30 miles along the shore of Chesapeake Bay, or join a survey of hurricane effects on the birds and vegetation in the tropical forests of Yucatan, Mexico.

Age range: 18 or over.
Children not accepted.
Qualifications: Good health. A medical statement from your physician is required.
Price range: $895 to $1,470.
Price includes: Field and research expenses, lab work, planning, accommodations, supplies, transportation. Meals vary by project.
Participants provide: Travel to site, visas, passports, additional living expenses.

190 Eco-Vacations

Sobek Expeditions

**PO Box 1089
Angels Camp CA 95222
Phone: (209)736-4524 Ext.23
Fax: (209)736-2646
Contact: Leslie Jarvie**

SOBEK has long been concerned about the preservation of rivers world-wide.

Its rafting trips emphasize the danger facing such rivers as the Tatshenshini in Alaska and Canada, threatened by mining and logging interests; the Bio-Bio of Chile, where a series of dams is planned; the Zambezi in Africa where a new dam is proposed; and the Grand Canyon of the Colorado, where careless operation of Glen Canyon Dam causes significant damage.

Environmental excursions focus on the wildlife, and cultural and environmental repercussions of rainforest destruction. You can travel by canoe into the Amazon Basin to experience a first-growth rainforest jungle. Here, you spend time in a biological reserve where river dolphins frolic in the clear water and tortoises sleep along the white sand beaches, and tour a model farm with agricultural products suited to rainforest ecology.

In Hawaii, you visit the Wao Kele O Puna Rainforest, one of the last existing lowland rainforests in the United States and site of a controversial geothermal power plant. This trip also spends time at sea to observe humpback whales and record their mating songs.

Other ecological trips explore the Mayan ruins in Belize; tour Rwanda and Zaire to see gorillas; and visit India to observe the one-horned rhino, wild buffalo, elephants, and tigers.

Age range: 16 to 80.
   Children under 18 are welcome.
Qualifications: None.
Price range: $150 a day.
Price includes: Accommodations, most meals, guides, transfers, internal transportation, park fees.
Participants provide: Airfare, personal items.

192 Eco-Vacations

Society Expeditions

**3131 Elliott Avenue/Suite 700
Seattle WA 98121
Phone: (800)426-7794/(206)285-9400
Fax: (206)285-7917
Contact: Erik Elvejord**

"This company is for the traveler who wants to participate in adventure and discover the world, not just sightsee," notes company president, Heiko Klein.

Society Expeditions has long been aware of the effects of tourism on the world. The company's nature travel programs use small expedition vessels which have the least impact when exploring a region because they are self-sufficient, and do not require hotels or tourist complexes on land.

Society Expeditions instituted Antarctica Visitor Guidelines to govern conduct in that fragile environment. These Guidelines have been reviewed by the National Science Foundation and accepted by North American Antarctic ship tour operators.

Organizations 193

Experienced naturalists lead all shore excursions, and remind travelers to observe the conservation ethic. Participants must not wander from paths, and must avoid camouflaged bird nests or fragile grasses.

Society Expeditions supports several preservation projects. Joining forces with the World Wildlife Fund in 1990, the company funds preservation projects in Indonesia and Madagascar.

You can visit some of these projects on Society Expeditions' tours and travel to Antarctica, the Amazon, the Gold Coast of Brazil, Polynesia, New Zealand, and Australia among other places.

Age range: 5 to 90.
Children 5 years and older are welcome.
Qualifications: None.
Price range: $300 a day.
Price includes: Cruise and hotel accommodations, most meals, shore excursions, tips, transfers, literature, lectures, expedition notebook and log of daily activities, leaders.
Participants provide: Airfare, personal items.

194 Eco-Vacations

Southern Cross Expeditions

PO Box 1228
Bowling Green Station
New York, NY 10274-1228
Phone: (800)359-0193
Fax: (516)287-1235
Contact: Raul Elizalde

Exploring South America is the specialty of this company, which emphasizes the physical and mental challenge of an adventure journey accompanied by naturalist guides from the region.

There's a walk along 80 miles of Brazil's southern Bahia beaches, to visit rustic coves, a national park, an Indian reserve, and untouched fishing village and coconut plantations. Another trek leads through Amazon jungle along a road opened by gold diggers to the base of Pico da Neblina, which is the highest point of Brazil but has never been climbed. You can explore the Pantanal region, a huge marshland area in Brazil near the Bolivian border, much like the Everglades in Florida.

Here you'll see crocodiles, giant storks which are the symbol of the area, monkeys, herons, parrots and other tropical birds.

You can choose a horseback crossing of the Andes; an exploration of the canyons of southern Brazil with unique wildlife and many bird species, led by a professor of biology; and a boat tour of the Submarine National Park of Abrolhos, 50 miles off the coast, to observe whales and sea birds, and to scuba dive in the coral reefs.

Age range: 20 to 60.
  Children under 18 accepted when accompanied by parents.
Qualifications: A medical questionnaire must be completed.
Price range: $1,200 to $3,150.
Price includes: Accommodations, most meals, transportation, transfers, trip leader, local guides, cooks, porters, helpers, pack animals, camping equipment, park/entrance fees, tips.
Participants pay: Airfare, passports, visas, insurance, alcoholic beverages, personal items.

196 Eco-Vacations

Student Conservation Association

PO Box 550
Charlestown NH 03603
Phone: (603)826-4301
Fax: (603)826-7755
Contact: Lesley Sullivan/Recruitment Director

So many people want to work on Student Conservation Association programs that there are often four applicants for every position available. The SCA was founded in 1957 as a nonprofit educational organization with three goals:

- to assist public and private groups in land and resource management by providing volunteers;
- to offer volunteers educational opportunities through conservation work;
- to involve the public in managing natural resources and increase public awareness of conservation.

Organizations 197

The Resource Assistant Program is designed for college students and adult volunteers. They serve for 12 to 16 weeks as assistants in national and state parks and forests, wildlife refuges and conservation areas. Most positions are with the National Park Service, US Forest Service, Bureau of Land Management, and US Fish and Wildlife Service. The work includes backcountry trail patrol, wildlife research, forest management, archaeological surveys, visitor information, and education.

The High School Program, aimed at students between 16 and 18, offers about 50 summer programs for more than 400 high school students. For up to five weeks, they çamp and work in national parks and forests.

Age range: 18 and over/Resource Assistant/16 to 18 in the High School Program.
Children under 16 not accepted.

Qualifications: Depends on position available.

Price range: Free. Most expenses (except travel in the High School program) covered by SCA.

Price includes: Accommodations, all meals OR food allowance of $45 a week, on-site training, supervision, travel expenses in Resource Assistant program, uniform grant.

Participants provide: Cost of additional meals, recreation, film, stamps, gas, personal items.

198 Eco-Vacations

Trans-Pacific Special Interest Tours

PO Box 30626
Santa Barbara CA 93130-0626
Phone: (805)682-6191
Fax: (805)682-4154
Contact: Ann L. Sween/Director

Expeditions to places of outstanding natural and cultural interest in the United States and abroad in cooperation with museums, botanic gardens, and other nonprofit organizations are the specialty of this company. Tours are led by expert guides and are designed for leisurely explorations.

There's a yacht tour of Canada's Queen Charlotte Islands, with visits to ancient Haida village sites. A cruise of Santa Barbara's Channel Islands spends three days looking for whales, porpoises, dolphins, and colonies of playful sea lions. An exploration of Steinbeck country visits Salina River Valley, Monterey Peninsula, and Big Sur in California.

A fall tour travels along the east coast to admire the autumn colors of Vermont, Massachusetts, and Canada.

Overseas, there's a trip to New Zealand, to see fjords, rain forests, towering snow-capped mountains, and glaciers, and learn about a culture shaped by Polynesian and European influences. Other tours visit the Canadian Arctic, Santa Fe, and Yellowstone National Park.

Age range: 55 to 80.
   Children under 18 welcome if accompanied by adults.
Qualifications: None.
Price range: $1,200 to $4,000.
Price includes: Airfare, transportation, accommodations, entrance fees, some meals, guides, specialists, donations to cooperating organizations.
Participants provide: Personal items.

University Research Expeditions Program

Desk MO-5
University of California
Berkeley CA 94720
Phone: (415)642-6586
Fax: (415)643-8683
Contact: Project Liaison

Nearly 4,000 volunteers have spent two to three weeks helping scientific discovery through UREP programs since they began in 1976. It's a unique opportunity to work with research scientists around the world on a variety of projects.

Volunteers help excavate sites of ancient Maya houses in Central America; document Hindu religious images in India; interview artists who design, carve, and paint masks in Bali and attend temple performances; join scuba divers to study the mating behavior of goby fish in French Polynesia; and observe seabirds in Baja, California, among scores of other programs.

Organizations 201

Projects are available year-round. Most expeditions have 6 to 10 members. Some projects are based in comfortable hotels in urban centers, while others involve camping in remote areas.

UREP sponsors projects in collaboration with scientists from developing countries in SHARE (Science Serving Humanity and Research for the Environment). These focus on improving people's lives and preserving the earth's resources. They include working with health professionals to collect data about children in the shantytowns of Brazil, where 35% of all infants die in their first year; or to assist in collecting plant samples and photographing habitats in Ecuador's disappearing rain forests.

Age range: 16 to 80+.
Children over 16 are accepted.
Qualifications: Enthusiasm, flexibility, able to be a team member, sense of humor.
Price range: $700 to $1,500. Contribution covers expenses to make the research possible. Teacher Research Participation Program offers grants to teachers in natural or social sciences.
Price includes: Accommodations, all meals, camping equipment, research equipment and supplies, field expenses, reading and pre-trip materials.
Participants provide: Airfare, travel costs to site, visas, passports, medical treatment, alcoholic beverages, personal items, sleeping bags.

202 Eco-Vacations

USDA Forest Service

324 25th Street
Ogden UT 84401
Phone: (801)625-5175
Fax: (801)625-5127
Contact: Regional Volunteer Coordinator

The Intermountain Region of the Forest Service invites volunteers to spend time helping to preserve the national forests in the states of Idaho, Nevada, Utah, and Wyoming.

A Volunteer Directory listing all openings is available in the spring. When you write or call for a copy of the Directory, mention *Eco-Vacations* and they will send you a free map of the Intermountain Region.

Those who are selected can serve as campground hosts, provide wilderness information programs in the parks, work on archaeological digs, assist with historical preservation projects, or work on a variety of other outdoor activities.

Age range: Adults.
Children under 18 if accompanied by parents.
Qualifications: Depends on the project.
Price range: No fee.
Participants provide: Travel, personal items.

204 Eco-Vacations

Volunteers for Peace

International Workcamps
43 Tiffany Road
Belmont VT 05730
Phone: (802)259-2759
Fax: (802)259-2922
Contact: Peter Coldwell

Working with people from different countries on environmental and cultural projects is the mission of Volunteers for Peace. Established in 1981, VFP has programs in 34 foreign and US communities. The majority are in Europe, and others are in Russia, Ghana, Tunisia, Morocco, India, and Turkey. Most run for two to three weeks between June and September.

A special program organized by the Earthstewards Network brings people between 18 and 23 from the USA, Russia, and Central America to plant thousands of trees along a river in Costa Rica. The project will counter the heavy erosion of years of over-cutting. Up to 400,000 seedlings are to be planted to reduce the loss of agricultural lands and stop the sediment run-off that causes the loss of fish habitats off the coast.

Organizations 205

Other outdoor projects take you to mark trails on mountain paths and to repair huts in the Appenine Mountains in Italy. You can weed and harvest on an farm in the Netherlands, repair winter storm damage in forests in Switzerland, or help build part of a long-distance path for cyclists and pedestrians in England.

On human relations projects, you assist in feeding the homeless in New York; build houses with Habitat in Connecticut; or help construct a school in Ghana.

The annual *International Workcamper Newsletter* and *International Workcamp Directory* give complete details of the programs. There are more than 700 listings of upcoming projects as well as a registration form and membership information. Ask for a free copy of the newsletter.

Age range: Most programs are for people over 18.
     Children over 16 sometimes accepted.
Qualifications: None.
Price range: $100 registration fee.
Price includes: Registration, room and board.
Participants provide: Airfare, transportation.

> *"Never have I found it so hard to leave a place. It was wonderful to be part of a close-knit group, and fascinating to discover the Asian elements of Siberian culture."*
>   US volunteer in Soviet Union.

206 Eco-Vacations

Washington State Senior Environmental Corps

Abbot Raphael Hall
Mailstop PV-11
Olympia WA 98504
Phone: (800)243-7890 in state
(206)438-7630
Fax: (206)459-6007
Contact: Pamela Jane Morgan

The Senior Environmental Corps was created in 1988 by Governor Booth Gardner to encourage seniors to share their training and skills with Washington State's Natural Resource agencies. These include the departments of Ecology, Fisheries, Parks, and Wildlife, and Puget Sound Water Quality Authority.

"It's an opportunity for people aged 55 and over to help preserve and protect our state's environment and natural resources," notes Pamela Morgan.

Organizations 207

Published bulletins list projects, location, type of experience needed, and starting dates, and describe the positions available.

Volunteers are offered a wide range of activities. They can help improve wildlife habitats, monitor wild turkey and elk, give safety and environmental presentations, and conduct shellfish surveys. They can staff information booths at boating and outdoor shows and answer environmental questions.

Other projects include developing recycling programs for small businesses, leading interpretive guided walks, and painting or photographing parks and natural scenery, monitoring water quality, or teaching youngsters about clean water.

Age range: 55 or older.
Children not accepted.
Qualifications: Must be 55 or older, professional or semi-professional, with suitable skills for project.
Price range: Free.
Price includes: Industrial insurance coverage, identifying hat, vest, nametag, information, and supplies to perform service, mileage reimbursement.
Participants provide: Transportation, personal items.

208 Eco-Vacations

Wild Horizons Expeditions

Dept ECO
West Fork Road
Darby MT 59829
Phone: (406)821-3747
Contact: Marilyn Olsen/Howie Wolke

You can travel through Jackson Hole and the Great Yellowstone region in Wyoming to be awed by rugged peaks, high plateaus, waterfalls, alpine lakes, and some of the largest big game herds in America. Or explore the Central Idaho/Western Montana wilderness, with towering icy summits, flower-strewn meadows, and rich river forests. Or hike along the trails of the Southwest to see Arizona's giant cacti, wildflowers, and desert reptiles, mammals, and birds.

This company now offers more than a dozen trips every year, with no more than eight participants on each trip.

The guides are all professionals in wilderness travel, and utilize safe, low-impact hiking and camping techniques. They're happy to teach participants wilderness skills. Family trips and custom trips for five days or more are also available.

Founded in 1978, WHE is a licensed guide and outfitter with the US Forest Service, National Park Service, and US Fish and Wildlife Service.

Age range: Teenagers to 70.
   Children under 18 are accepted.
Qualifications: Good physical condition is essential; hikers should be able to carry a 30- to 40-lb. pack over rugged terrain, and travel about seven miles a day.
Price range: $585 to $795.
Price includes: Accommodations, all meals, naturalist guide, backpack, daypack, tent, sleeping bag, pad, water bottle, utensils, transportation to trailhead and back.
Participants provide: Airfare, personal items.

210 Eco-Vacations

Wilderness Southeast

711 Sandtown Road
Savannah GA 31410
Phone:(912)897-5108
Contact: Director

"We interpret nature, we don't control it," is the philosophy of Wilderness Southeast, a nonprofit outdoor school which has been taking adults and teenagers to Florida, Georgia, Costa Rica, Belize, the Bahamas, and the coasts of South Carolina and Georgia since 1973.

Choose a canoe trip in the Okefenokee Swamp to see the alligators and the giant cypress trees, and travel on to the tupelo gum trees and spectacular white sand beaches of the Suwannee River. Hike and camp in the Great Smoky Mountains. Visit Georgia's Cumberland Island to walk along sandy trails and nearly deserted beaches. Spend a leisurely week cruising through the Everglades while you live on a houseboat.

Most trips develop skills for exploring both natural and cultural environments. All programs follow minimum-impact camping procedures. Groups have no more than

Organizations 211

16 people, and everyone shares camp chores.

"The most important thing to bring on any program is your cheerful acceptance of whatever surprise the wilderness may hold," advises the staff.

Special teenage programs offer a marine science camp in Georgia; a backpack trip in the Shining Rock Wilderness area; and a sailing and camping trip to the tropical island reefs in the British Virgin Islands.

Age range: 8 to 80.
Children under 18 welcome on most programs.
Qualifications: A few on specific trips.
Price range: $260 to $1,500.
Price includes: Driving map to location, instructors, all meals, tent space, cooking and camping equipment, canoe equipment, transportation, reference library, first aid, safety equipment.
Participants provide: Airfare, canteen, personal items. Sleeping bag, pad, daypack, duffle bag; snorkel gear can be rented.

"This trip increased my love for the ocean and the possibility for me to be a marine biologist."
A teenager

212 Eco-Vacations

Wildlands Studies

San Francisco State University
3 Mosswood Circle
Cazadero CA 95421
Phone: (707)632-5665
Contact: Crandall Bay/Director

If you're interested in studying grizzly bears in Yellowstone, bobcats in Georgia, whales in Canada, or wolves in Idaho, there are several wildlife projects where volunteer help is needed.

Wildlands Studies participants become part of backcountry study teams of no more than 12 members and help researchers find answers to environmental problems. They work as associates out in the field with others from the United States and Canada.

A project in New Zealand studies the country's environmental programs as well as the conflicts and cooperation among European and Polynesian residents.

In Canada, scientists observe the behavior, foraging strategies, and migration patterns of whales in the St.

Organizations 213

Lawrence Estuary. Other projects examine the ecosystems of Baja, China's vanishing forests, and conservation and development in Nepal.

"At times, research can be frustrating, repetitious, or just plain hard work. But it is also a rare and fascinating opportunity to explore our wildlands firsthand while striving toward shared goals with experienced researchers and new friends," notes Crandall Bay.

Age range: 18 and above.
Children under 18 not accepted.
Qualifications: All necessary skills are taught on-site by resource specialists. A statement of health is required of all applicants.
Price range: $385 to $775.
Price includes: Participation in field research study, equipment, instruction.
Participants provide: Travel to site, shared costs of food and on-site transportation, backpacking equipment, personal items.

214 Eco-Vacations

Womantrek

**1411 E Olive Way
PO Box 20643
Seattle WA 08102
Phone: (800)477-TREK/(206)325-4772
Fax: (206)324-2512
Contact: Bonnie Bordas**

"Travel is one of the most expanding, enriching experiences in life. We can explore fragile ecosystems, raft wild rivers, and discover hidden waterfalls. We can leave the well-worn tourist paths behind and travel right into the heart of exotic, far-flung cultures," Bonnie Bordas explains.

She began Womantrek with the first women's cycling tour of East China in May 1983, which proved so successful that Bordas now offers women scores of biking, hiking, rafting, sailing, and cultural trips.

She'll take you rafting through the Grand Canyon, or down the Main Salmon River in Idaho. You can hike in Oregon's Hells Canyon and Eagle Cap, and through Washington's North Cascades mountains.

Abroad, you can trek in Peru, Kashmir, Sikkim, Nepal, and Tibet. There are safaris in Africa and a yacht cruise of the Caribbean. Groups are usually fewer than 15 women.

Bordas believes that women enjoy the challenge of the outdoors as much as men, and prove themselves able to accomplish amazing feats when offered the opportunity. Her background includes working for Outward Bound as an instructor.

All guides are women, selected for their expertise and knowledge. In Sikkim, for example, the leader is Daku Tensing Norgay, who owns and manages a trekking company in India. In Kashmir, Karalyn Kana, an American art historian, leads treks based on her extensive experience there.

Age range: 21 to 72.
Children under 18 not accepted.
Qualifications: Women only.
Price range: $55 to $3,500.
Price includes: Accommodations, transportation, guides, sightseeing, and most meals.
Participants provide: Airfare, travel insurance, personal items.

"This trip gave me a sense of myself as a woman and not as the second half of a couple."
A participant

216 Eco-Vacations

World Wildlife Fund

1250 24th Street NW
Washington DC 20037
Phone: (202)778-9683/(202)293-4800
Fax: (202)293-9211
Contact: Janet Fesler;
Katherine Anthony/Travel

WWF is the largest private US organization working worldwide to conserve nature. More than a million Americans are members. The WWF has supported more than 3,000 projects in close to 145 countries since its founding in 1961.

The Fund's aims include:
· protecting natural areas and wild populations of plants and animals, including endangered species;
· promoting sustainable approaches to the use of renewable natural resources; and
· promoting more efficient use of resources and energy and the maximum reduction of pollution.

To help members understand the challenges of ecology and conservation, WWF offers trips led by a naturalist and WWF staff. For example, a tour of the tropical rain forests of the Caribbean island of Dominica takes participants not only to see some of the 162 native species of birds but also to visit one of the last settlements of the Carib people, and to explore the WWF Forest Conservation Project.

Other trips visit Australia, Antarctica, Costa Rica, the Galapagos Islands, Argentina, Zimbabwe, Kenya, Botswana, and Alaska's Inside Passage.

Age range: Adults.
   Children under 18 are not encouraged.
Qualifications: Good health; fitness level for destination.
Price range: $1,700 to $10,000.
Price includes: Airfare from gateway city on most trips, transportation, accommodations, most meals, airport taxes, local guides, tips, entrance fees, leadership, pre-trip materials.
Participants provide: Airfare to gateway city, extra beverages or food, immunizations, passport, insurance, personal items.

218 Eco-Vacations

Yellowstone Institute

Box 117
Yellowstone National Park
Wyoming 82190
Phone: (307)344-7381/Ext.2384
Contact: Registrar

Driving through the magnificent wilderness of Yellowstone National Park in Wyoming is one way to see it. But to gain a better understanding of its ecology, combine your visit with one of the Yellowstone Institute's 70 classes. These cover more than 25 different topics, from llama packing to flyfishing to grizzly bears, and are led by qualified experts.

Among programs offered is a seminar on Indian use of Yellowstone and tribal migrations, traditional roles of men and women, trails, and treaties. It is led by Jeanne M. Eder, a member of the Sioux tribe, who explains the roles of folklore and religion in the natural environment of Yellowstone.

Other programs study the ecological relationships of birds in the park to see how environment and habitat

Organizations 219

affect the red crossbill, bald eagle, osprey, and white pelican, among others. Canoeing across Lewis and Shoshone Lakes for five days emphasizes low-impact backcountry camping techniques.

The Institute has two classrooms in a log building. Students stay in cabins with no plumbing, heating, or electricity, and bring their own food to cook in a communal kitchen. They can also stay at campgrounds in the park, or in nearby hotels or motels.

Most classes include field trips, so participants should be prepared for mountain weather with possible cold temperatures or rain.

Age range: 18 to 75.
Children accepted at children and family classes.
Qualifications: None.
Price range: $35 per day.
Price includes: Class and instruction.
Participants provide: Transportation, $7 per night cabin fee, food, sleeping bags.

220 Eco-Vacations

Zoar Outdoors

PO Box 245
Mohawk Trail
Charlemont MA 01339
Phone: (413)339-4010
Contact: Bruce Lessels

Situated in the Deerfield River Valley of the Berkshires, Zoar Outdoors organizes raft, canoe, and mountain climbing programs in Vermont and northwestern Massachusetts as an introduction to the wilderness areas of the region.

Instruction in canoeing, kayaking, and rafting is given by qualified instructors, plus a special racing clinic for intermediate and advanced paddlers.

If you'd prefer a more leisurely introduction to the wilderness, take a one-day canoe or raft trip along the Mohawk Trail on the Deerfield River.

Age range: 7 to 99.
  Children under 18 are welcome.
Qualifications: None.
Price range: $39 to $210.
Price includes: Meals, guide, instruction. Canoes, paddles, lifejackets, wetsuits can be rented. Accommodations available with some activities.
Participants provide: Transportation, personal items.

Zoetic Research

Sea Quest Expeditions
PO Box 2424F
Friday Harbor WA 98250
Phone: (206)378-5767
Contact: Mark Lewis

"Sea kayaks create an intimate bond between paddler and ocean. Gliding silently across the water's surface in your kayak, you should absorb the sea's pulse through the paddle and hull. Like the salmon and orca whale, you feel compelled to respond to complex rhythms of wave, current, and tide. These primeval sensations have been experienced by kayakers for centuries," notes Mark Lewis, Expeditions Director.

Mark Lewis has been a sea kayak guide for seven years. He is also the senior author of a book on the birds of the Washington's San Juan Archipelago, and a research associate of the Whale Museum in Friday Harbor.

All Zoetic Research trips, which last from one to seven days, are led by qualified biologists.

You paddle in two-person fiberglass kayaks with foot-controlled rudders. You can explore the San Juan Islands of the Pacific Northwest, Mexico's Baja Peninsula, or the Everglades and Dry Tortugas of Florida.

On some programs, you assist biologists on whale research projects.

Zoetic means "endowed with life" which reflects the spirit of these expeditions. Zoetic Research is a nonprofit organization dedicated to scientific research, environmental education, and conservation of natural resources.

Age range: 12 and up.
   Children under 18 are welcome if well-behaved.
Qualifications: Interest in kayaking.
Price range: $45 to $899.
Price includes: Accommodations, transportation, kayaks, equipment, all meals, guides.
Participants provide: Airfare, sleeping bag, personal items.

224 Eco-Vacations

Appendix 225

Appendix

National Audubon Society Travel Ethic for Environmentally Responsible Tourism

Tourism is one of the fastest growing industries in the world today. In some countries, so far little-known to travelers, where there are huge problems of unemployment and weak national economies, tourism is being regarded as a new primary industry. It creates employment and often brings in foreign currency to economically marginal areas. Sightseers from more affluent nations are ever searching for new places to explore. The trend seems to be growing away from sun, sea, and sand holidays toward adventure, the outdoors, wildlife watching, and cultural interests.

Close encounters with members of the animal kingdom are at very high interest levels. This coincides with a rapidly developing public awareness of environmental matters. Such a combination of conditions could lead to an influx of excursionists into environmentally sensitive areas which, if not carefully managed, could exert pressure and do possibly irrevocable damage to the natural resources it seeks.

226 Eco-Vacations

The National Audubon Society realizes that the maintenance of these sensitive resources will ensure the continuation of tourism in such areas. The resource in question is the entire natural world, from coastal Alaska and the high Arctic and Greenland, to the wilderness of Antarctic and all that lies between.

The National Audubon Society has become increasingly aware of both the potential and actual conflict between tourism development and the natural environment. We are completely convinced that more can be done to create a positive balance between the two and to create an atmosphere where commercial operators and environmentalists can interact positively. We recognize that tourism can be a powerful tool favoring environmental conservation -- particularly through enhancement of public awareness of environmentally sensitive areas and their resources and the stimulation of action and mobilization of support to prevent the erosion of such environments.

Toward these goals, the National Audubon Society urges all tour operators promoting exploration in wilderness areas to adopt the guidelines here stated.

Appendix 227

Guidelines

1. Wildlife and their habitats must not be disturbed.

2. Audubon tourism to natural areas will be sustainable.

3. Waste disposal must have neither environmental nor aesthetic impacts.

4. The experience a tourist gains in traveling with Audubon must enrich his or her appreciation of nature, conservation, and the environment.

5. Audubon Tours must strengthen the conservation effort and enhance the natural the natural integrity of places visited.

6. Traffic in products that threaten wildlife and plant populations must not occur.

7. The sensibilities of other cultures must be respected.

228 Eco-Vacations

What the Guidelines Mean

1. Wildlife and their habitats must not be disturbed.

Fragile habitats must not be stressed. Trails will be followed. Plants will be left to grow.

In delicate habitats, vegetation destruction and rock slides can easily be caused by the trampling of too many people. Mosses, lichens, and certain wildflowers and grasses may take as much as 100 years to more to regenerate, and must not be walked upon. It is the obligation of the tour company and the naturalist leaders to promote a "stay on the trail" policy. No responsible tour operator or naturalist should allow the removal or picking of plant specimens or other ground cover. Introduction of exotic plan species must be avoided.

Coral reefs take anywhere from several years to several decades to regenerate. Therefore, the National Audubon Society insists that all of its tour operators provide the broadest protection possible for this underwater life form. Destruction of any part of any coral reef calls for the greatest censure.

Appendix 229

Animal behavior will not be inhibited. Because many of the most well-subscribed tours are operated during various animals' breeding season, tour operators and leaders should establish and always maintain at least minimum distance from these animals.

Scientific studies predict that a specific animal behavioral function, such as courtship, nesting, or feeding young, demands a specific amount of energy on the part of the breeding animal. Approaching animals too closely causes them to expend energy needlessly in a fury of defensive territorial display. This can cause an energy deficit that reduces the animals' productivity in the same way as does a food shortage. If disturbances are caused by visitors early enough in the breeding cycle, the parents may abandon the breeding site. Additionally, while the adults are warding off intruders, eggs and young are vulnerable to chilling, and unguarded young are more susceptible to predation.

Animals will not be harassed or approached too closely. Our recommendation is that all tour participants keep a minimum distance of 20-to-30-feet from seals, walruses, otters, giant tortoises, lava lizards, sea turtles, koalas, all marsupials, and unwary plains herd animals.

We recommend that all visitors stay on the periphery of animal assemblages e.g. penguin colonies, seabird

230 Eco-Vacations

colonies, terneries, albatrosses on nest, courting groups, etc. This means:

- Visitors should never be allowed to surround an animal or group of animals.
- Visitors and leaders must remain alert never to get between animal parents and their young.
- Visitors must never be allowed to get between marine mammals and the water's edge.
- Nesting raptors should be viewed only through binoculars or telescopes at considerable distances from the nest.
- Crowd control ethics include keeping the decibel level as low as possible, thereby minimizing the potential threat to animals.
- The advent of sophisticated photographic technology means that even amateur photographers can get professional-looking photographs while keeping a respectable distance from the subject. Photography of birds and animals should never include the removal of nestlings or young from the nest or removal of foliage or camouflage from close to the breeding site. Removal of animals from burrows, dens, caves, or tree cavities must be prohibited at all times.
- Relentlessly following or harassing birds or animals for the sake of a photograph should never be allowed. Lingering obtrusively in close proximity to a nesting site, preventing the animal from returning to the site, should never be allowed.
- Touching animals must never be allowed.

Appendix 231

Every effort will be made to minimize a visit's impact, and if that effort is inadequate, the visit will be curtailed.

2. Audubon tourism to natural areas will be sustainable.

Audubon will encourage local guides, landowners, and conservation representatives to develop and implement long-term visitor plans to ensure the sustainable use of their wildlife habitats. Audubon also encourages patronage of locally benign concessionaires.

3. Waste disposal must have neither environmental nor aesthetic impacts.

All tour operators must take into account the fragility of the areas visited with regard to proper waste disposal. All cruise ships, whether operating in the Arctic or sub-Arctic, the Great Barrier Reef of Australia, the islands of the Southern Ocean, along the Antarctic Peninsula, the Pacific shores of South America and Galapagos, or along the reaches of the Orinoco and Amazon rivers must commit to a shipboard anti-dumping/anti-garbage policy. This policy ensures that the shpboard crew and staff will not foul any waters, particularly with regard to non-biodegradable (plastic) materials.

232 Eco-Vacations

If necessary, all trash must be contained and carried back to a port where proper disposal is available. Any tour operator offering the opportunity for visiting land wildernesss areas overnight or for several days must make provision for carrying out all trash generated while there.

The tour operator and naturalists should promote an attitude of keeping every specific site as clean as possible. No littering of any kind should be tolerated.

The National Audubon Society will neither patronize nor approve any vendor that does not *strictly* adhere to this guideline.

4. The experience a tourist gains in traveling with Audubon must enrich his or her appreciation of nature, conservation, and the environment.

Every trip to a wilderness area must be led by experienced, well-trained, responsible naturalists and guides. These naturalists should have a solid background in the various habitats to be visited, the flora and fauna contained there, and the sensitive nature of those habitats. These naturalists and guides must be able to provide proper supervision of the visitors, prevent disturbances to the area, answer questions of the visitors regarding the flora and fauna of the area, and present the conservation issues relevant to the area.

Appendix 233

All tour operators should provide adequate space for these naturalists so that the leader-to-group size ratio never exceeds one to 25. The maximum size of a visiting group will depend upon the fragility of the surroundings, in which case the ratio could drop to as little as one to ten.

These naturalist/guides serve as the environmental conscience of the group and as such should be an integral part of every tour.

5. *Audubon Tours must strengthen the conservation effort and enhance the natural integrity of places visited.*

One constant theme in Audubon tours will be the problems facing wildlife and their habitat, and the solutions that may be achieved. On tours particularly to other countries, contacts will be sought and established with conservation organizations working in the areas visited. Their representatives will be encouraged to speak to our tours and sought, when appropriate, to serve as local naturalist leaders and lecturers to accompany Audubon en route.

6. *Traffic in products that threaten wildlife and plant populations must not occur.*

The National Audubon Society cannot condone a laissez-faire attitude with regard to purchase of certain

234 Eco-Vacations

types of souvenirs or mementoes. Habitat loss remains the single largest threat to animal species; however, commerce and poaching have also depleted countless animal and plant populations. All our vendors must conscientiously educate their travelers against buying the following items:
- All sea turtle products, including jewelry, sea turtle eggs, skin cream made from turtle meat;
- Most reptile skins and leathers, particularly those from Latin America, the Caribbean, China, Egypt (including all crocodile products);
- Snakeskin products from Latin America and Asian countries, including India;
- Lizardskin products from Brazil, Paraguay, India, Nepal, and Pakistan;
- Leather products made of pangolin (anteater) from Thailand, Malaysia, and Indonesia;
- Ivory from any source, especially worked ivory from elephants and marine mammals, such as whales, walruses, and narwhals;
- Birds, including large parrots from Australia, Brazil, Ecuador, Paraguay, Venezuela, and the Caribbean islands;
- Wild birds and their feathers and skins, used in or as artwork (including mounted birds);
- Coral from Caribbean, SE Asia, Australia;
- Furs of spotted cats e.g. snow leopard, jaguar, ocelot, etc.

Appendix 235

- Furs and fur products of seals and other marine mammals and polar bears;
- Any orchids and cacti.

7. The sensibilities of other cultures must be respected.

Audubon tours travel in areas of widely varying ethics and practices. On our trips we are the guests of these cultures and our opportunities are to learn and enrich our own understanding of human nature, not to intrude and criticize. In the long run, our abilities to advance conservation will be strengthened by the bridges that understanding will establish.

* * * * * * * * * * *

The effectiveness of the preceding guidelines rests on the performances and cooperation of the tour operator, the naturalist leaders, and the expedition travelers. Each of these parties must possess and promote a sense of propriety if the collective effort is to succeed. Harmless viewing of wildlife and habitats in which wildlife abounds can proliferate while preserving both the activity and the resource.

Copyright 1989 National Audubon Society Inc.
All rights reserved. Reprinted with permission.

236 Eco-Vacations

Index

air pollution 3, 16, 19, 20, 156
Alaska 7, 8, 23, 32, 38, 44, 47, 50, 53, 54, 57, 61-63,
77, 80, 81, 92, 93, 108, 133, 139, 149, 161,
169, 180, 190, 217
Amazon 111, 132, 149, 163, 164, 169, 180, 190, 193,
194
Anasazi 25, 104, 106
Antarctic 47, 192
Appalachian 21, 29, 32, 44, 51, 54, 58, 76
archaeology 3, 19, 25, 97, 106, 107, 134, 135, 156
architecture 26
Arctic 23, 26, 32, 36, 39, 42, 44, 47, 51, 54, 58,
78-81, 92, 154, 199
astronomy 82
Australia 4, 22, 31, 50, 64, 86, 109, 153, 169, 181,
193, 217
Avignon 140
backpack 15, 62, 66, 135, 209, 211
Bahia 194
Baja 8, 23, 32, 39, 47, 54, 83, 88, 89, 169, 200, 213,
223
Bali 22, 86, 153, 173, 200
bears 22, 63, 79, 92, 154, 161, 186, 212, 218
Belize 132, 136, 137, 169, 191, 210
Berkshires 77, 220
bicycle 20, 21, 23, 26, 27, 29, 32, 33, 36, 45, 47, 48,
51, 54, 58, 86, 87, 122, 123, 128, 130, 131
biking 8, 9, 16, 20, 44, 74, 214

238 *Eco-Vacations*

birding 16, 136, 174
birds 3, 9, 19, 22, 38, 53, 64, 80, 90, 105, 116, 133, 146, 155, 162, 177, 181, 189, 195, 208, 217, 218, 222
botany 42, 83, 105, 106
Brazil 24, 30, 43, 49, 52, 55, 124, 164, 193-195, 201
bromeliads 137
Brooks Range 80, 81
buffalo 140, 191
building 8, 26, 77, 126, 168, 219
business 61, 177
cacti 208
California 7, 20, 23, 32, 38, 39, 42, 47, 50, 54, 75, 83, 86, 90, 111, 144, 187, 198, 200
camel 153, 187
camping 8, 13, 16, 44, 57, 62, 63, 73, 75, 83, 86, 97, 119, 135, 139, 144, 145, 153, 174, 187, 195, 201, 208, 210, 211, 219
Canada 4, 64, 75, 94, 160, 161, 190, 198, 199, 212, 226
canoe 8, 9, 21, 23, 26, 32, 39, 45, 53, 54, 58, 62, 63, 94-96, 116, 147, 190, 210, 211, 220
Cape Cod 4, 22, 130, 131, 171
China 47, 69, 86, 139, 149, 150, 153, 213, 214
cities 3, 7, 19, 25, 26, 28, 100, 153, 156, 178
Colorado 6, 9, 25, 32, 38, 44, 45, 51, 54, 58, 69, 73, 81, 96, 102, 107, 158, 163, 187, 190
conservation 20, 21, 24, 27, 30, 34, 40, 43, 46, 52, 55, 59, 70, 72, 76, 82, 144, 148, 149, 158, 159, 169, 172, 173, 176, 184, 193, 196, 197, 213, 216, 217, 223
coral reef 31, 146, 147
Costa Rica 83, 89, 132, 148, 150, 151, 153, 169, 180, 189, 204, 210, 217
Czechoslovakia 28, 153

Index 239

```
dinosaur  . . . . . . . . . . . . . . . . . . . . . . . . . . . . . . . .  120
disabilities  . . . . . . . . . . . . . . . . . . . . . . . . . .  150, 151, 174
dolphins  . . . . . . . .  16, 22, 38, 64, 73, 113, 168, 169, 190, 198
Dominica . . . . . . . . . . . . . . . . . . . . . . . . . . . . . . . . .  217
eagles  . . . . . . . . . . . . . . . . . . . . . . . . . . .  63, 80, 166, 167
economics  . . . . . . . . . . . . . . . . . . . . . . . . . . . . . . . .  177
Ecuador  . . . . . . . . . . . . . . . . . . . . . . .  4, 132, 153, 201
education . . . . . . . .  14, 74, 104, 110, 114, 118, 132, 146, 154,
                    156, 158, 162, 166, 168, 177, 184, 197, 223
elephants . . . . . . . . . . . . . . . . . . . . . . . . .  50, 134, 172, 191
England . . . . . . .  4, 26, 31, 44, 47, 77, 86, 130, 131, 150, 187,
                                                              205
Fiji . . . . . . . . . . . . . . . . . . . . . . . . . . . . . . . . . . . .  184
flamingoes . . . . . . . . . . . . . . . . . . . . . . . . . . . . . . . .  133
Florida  . . . . . . .  22, 23, 26, 29, 31, 32, 39, 42, 45, 51, 54, 58,
                    73, 105, 114, 116, 117, 146, 171, 194, 210,
                                                              223
flowers  . . . . . . . . . . . . . . . . . . . . . . .  3, 19, 31, 50, 80, 113
France . . . . . . . . . . . . . .  4, 26, 69, 71, 86, 130, 131, 140, 141
Galapagos  . . . . . . . . .  4, 31, 38, 111, 149, 161, 163, 173, 217
geology  . . . . . . . . . . . . . . . . . . . . . . . . .  71, 83, 105, 175
Georgia . . . . . . . . . . . . . . . . . . . . . . . . . . . .  9, 210-212
gorillas  . . . . . . . . . . . . . . . . . . . . . . . . . . . . . .  71, 191
Grand Canyon  . . . . . . . .  4, 20, 38, 53, 82, 83, 135, 183, 190,
                                                              214
Hawaii  . . . . . . .  4, 31, 44, 53, 70, 72, 86, 112, 113, 139, 153,
                                                    163, 169, 173, 191
health care . . . . . . . . . . . . . . . . . . . . . . . . . . . . . . . .  177
high school . . . . . . . . . . . . . . . . . . . . . . . . . . . .  107, 197
hiking  . . . . . . . . .  8, 12, 16, 23, 26, 32, 36, 39, 42, 44, 50, 54,
                    57, 63, 66, 67, 74, 81, 102, 139, 145, 159,
                                                    175, 187, 208, 214
Himalayas  . . . . . . . . . . . . . . . . . . . . . .  138, 139, 152, 172
history . . . . . . . .  3, 10, 19, 23, 25, 26, 29, 32, 39, 42, 44, 47,
                    50, 54, 58, 67, 70, 93, 95, 100, 105, 109,
                    114, 132, 136, 141, 146, 148, 149, 162-164,
                                                         174, 185
```

240 Eco-Vacations

horseshoe crab 22
human relations 3, 19, 35, 184, 205
Hungary 28
Ice Age 71
Idaho 66, 83, 86, 183, 187, 189, 202, 208, 212, 214
Inca 138, 163
India 9, 35, 50, 118, 119, 139, 153, 163, 173, 191,
                                          200, 204, 215
Indian 97, 114, 116, 118, 163, 180, 188, 194, 218
internships 21, 24, 27, 29, 33, 36, 39, 42, 46, 51, 55,
                                          66, 68, 156, 157
Ireland 154, 182
Italy 4, 26, 35, 69, 86, 122, 140, 150, 205
Jamaica 188, 189
kayak 62, 88, 222
Kenya 128, 129, 152, 162, 169, 185, 217
Kerala 118
llamas 73, 144, 145
Louisiana 44, 86
lynx 80
macaws 91, 137
Madagascar 162, 193
Maine 77, 86, 104, 187
Maya 200
mediaeval 26, 140
Mexico 4, 7, 20, 22, 26, 64, 72, 86, 96, 104, 120,
                                  121, 124, 136, 142, 163, 189, 223
Minnesota 53, 94
Mississippi 68
monkeys 22, 91, 134, 137, 195
Montana 44, 120, 158, 180, 189, 208
musk ox 80
Nepal 139, 152, 173, 213, 215
New Hampshire 77
New Jersey 20, 44, 67

Index 241

New Mexico 20, 86, 96, 104, 120, 163
New Zealand 4, 71, 72, 86, 105, 181, 183, 193, 199, 212
North Carolina 86, 158
North Pole 78, 79
Ohio 142
orchids 137
Oregon 44, 86, 111, 155, 174, 183, 214
owls 80, 167
painting 16, 207
parrots 22, 137, 195
peace 7, 21, 27, 30, 34, 35, 37, 40, 43, 46, 49, 52, 56, 83, 128, 182, 204
pelicans 22, 90
Peru 72, 132, 134, 138, 152, 163, 173, 215
photographing 201, 207
polar bears 79, 154, 161
pollution 3, 16, 19, 20, 28, 86, 90, 100, 156, 216
Polynesia 193, 200
population 21, 29, 36, 40, 41, 46, 136, 137, 178, 179
prairie dog 120
rainforest 31, 57, 132, 164, 165, 190, 191
recycling 20, 207
research 3, 6, 14, 16, 19, 22-24, 26, 27, 29, 30, 33, 34, 36, 37, 39, 40-46, 48-52, 54-56, 58, 59, 61, 65, 108-112, 114, 115, 120, 132, 134-136, 149, 165, 169, 177, 184, 186, 188, 189, 197, 200, 201, 213, 222, 223
rhinos 172
river-rafting 38, 96
rock art 97, 120
Russia 47, 151, 204
Rwanda 71, 191
sailing 8, 14, 21, 36, 38, 40, 46, 48, 59, 100, 112, 113, 146, 170, 171, 183, 211, 214
scientists 8, 10, 16, 108, 120, 134, 148, 200, 201, 212
Scotland 4, 154, 181, 187

242 Eco-Vacations

sealions 64, 88, 163
seals 64, 133, 160, 161
Sierra Leone 121
Sioux 218
South Africa 124
South Carolina 22, 210
Stockholm 28, 176
Tanzania 71, 152, 162, 169
teenage 159, 211
Thailand 69, 86, 139, 153, 185
trekking 57, 144, 173, 215
Tunisia 128, 204
Turkey 38, 173, 204, 207
turtles 9, 121, 137, 148, 149
Utah 38, 83, 96, 187, 202
Venezuela 90, 133, 180
Vermont 86, 158, 199, 220
Wales 26, 121
walking 8, 26, 71, 148, 152, 174, 177
whales 8, 16, 38, 63-65, 88, 113, 133, 134, 169, 191, 195, 198, 212
wildflowers 8, 31, 97, 181, 208
wolves 167, 212
women 14, 124, 171, 182, 183, 214, 215, 218
Wyoming 77, 180, 183, 187, 202, 208, 218

Notes

ORDER FORM

Yes, send a copy of *Eco-Vacations: Enjoy Yourself and Save the Earth* to:

NAME..

ADDRESS..

....

STATE/ZIP..

PHONE............................

PRICE: $22.50 + $2.50 for shipping = $25.00

ADD $10 shipping for CANADA and outside US.

Enclosed is my check for $......... for ..... copy/ies Send
to BLUE PENGUIN PUBLICATIONS
 BPP/Sales
 147 Sylvan Avenue
 Leonia NJ 07605

ALL ORDERS PREPAID.
Please allow 4 weeks for delivery.
Thank you.

ISBN 0-9626231-1-3
Library of Congress No: 91-070296

ORDER FORM for TRAVEL AND LEARN

TRAVEL AND LEARN:
The New Guide to Educational Travel, 1990 Edition.
Blue Penguin Publications.
A lively informative guide which provides complete details of more than 1,000 educational vacation programs in the United States and abroad offered by universities, colleges, museums and educational organizations. Reviewers said: *"For the inveterate traveler, this book is perfect"* and *"The range of topics is amazing."*

PRICE: $23.95 plus $2.05 for shipping. TOTAL: $26.00
Send me _____ copy/ies of TRAVEL AND LEARN.

NAME...

ADDRESS..

....

Enclosed is my check for $_____
Send to: Sales Department,
       Blue Penguin Publications,
       147 Sylvan Avenue, Leonia NJ 07605.
Please allow 4 weeks for delivery.

ISBN 0-9626231-0-5.
Library of Congress No: 90-81540